THE BLUE PLAQUE GUIDE TO LONDON HOMES

QUEEN ANNE PRESS

THE
BLUE PLAQUE
GUIDE
TO LONDON HOMES

MARTIN HALL

LONDON

ISBN 0362 00287 8

Designed by **Pete Pengilley**
Photographs of houses by **Julian Plowright**

First published in 1976 by **Queen Anne Press Ltd**
12 Vandy Street London EC2A 2EN

Filmset in Monophoto Ionic by
BAS Printers Limited, Wallop, Hampshire

Printed in Great Britain by
Fletcher & Son, Norwich

Front cover illustrations:
Left Sir Charles Barry's house at The Elms, Clapham Common North, SW4
Centre Charles Dickens' plaque at 48 Doughty Street, WC1
Right Thomas Carlyle, whose statue is near his house at 24 Cheyne Row, SW3

Back cover illustrations:
Left Dante Gabriel Rossetti's house at 16 Cheyne Walk, SW3
Right The house where George Eliot died, at 4 Cheyne Walk, SW3

ACKNOWLEDGEMENTS

My thanks are due first and foremost to Mr Frank Bailey, who, although a busy executive in motion pictures, gave me the initial idea for this book, and encouraged me throughout its writing by his enormous insight into London's past. I am indebted also to Julian Plowright for the excellence of his photographs; to Anne Mitchell for her help and assistance as my picture researcher, and to the librarians in the reference sections of many boroughs in London, in particular Kensington, Chelsea and Westminster. My thanks also to Mr Louis Bondy, the Chairman of the Historic Buildings Board, for his kind assistance and enthusiasm towards this book. My deep thanks to my father, Dr Gilbert Hall, for the use of his superb collection of books in his Sussex home and finally, my gratitude is due to Rosalie Vicars-Harris, my editor at Queen Anne Press, for her kindness, consideration and patience throughout the preparation of this book.

M.H.

CONTENTS

Fashionable Londoners of the 1860s promenading in Kensington Gardens, as drawn by Walter Crane.

FOREWORD

Blue Plaques are as much part of London as the pigeons. If a plaque cannot actually perch on the nose of one of Frederick Leighton's lions in Trafalgar Square, it can and does decorate the façade of Lord Leighton's house in Kensington. Hanging in the National Portrait Gallery is a painting of Leighton carving his lion. And now in this delightful book we can read about what happened behind the scenes in Leighton's house, where he worked and received his fashionable guests. This is Martin Hall's purpose throughout his *Blue Plaque Guide to London Homes*: to tell us what went on behind the smooth azure circles with the elegant white lettering.

All of us who grew up in London, as I did, will have our special Blue Plaque fantasies. The first movie I ever saw was a penguin spectacular which for me meant my hero Scott of the Antarctic. When I later saw his Blue Plaque at the bottom of Oakley Street by Chelsea Embankment, I at once visualised a fur-clad figure banging the front door of his tall brick house, whistling up his team of huskies, and sailing down the Thames to fame and death. Martin Hall's researches are a good deal more authentic than my daydreams, but no less evocative to me of London's living past.

Painters and writers respond particularly well to Martin Hall's 'home' treatment, since they did the actual work for which they are famous on the spot now marked for posterity. I am enchanted to hear of Sir John Millais throwing open the double doors of his studio in Palace Gate, and ordering a little inspirationary music. Did the fair pianist in the next room temper her notes to the distinguished sitter? Church music, perhaps, for Mr Gladstone, and Lord Byron's *Hebrew Melodies* for Lord Beaconsfield. I can add an inside touch to the poetess Christina Rossetti's house in Torrington Square, culled from *Chapters from Childhood* by her niece Juliet Soskice. Aunt Christina would sit in the backroom in a black dress and white cap, 'with her hands folded, thinking and waiting'—not for poetic inspiration but—'for the kettle to boil'. She kept sweets in a big cupboard, goldfish in a tank, and two ancient, ugly aunts in the upstairs bedroom. She made Juliet a tiny dining-room table and chairs out of chestnuts, modelled on her own at Torrington Square.

Blue Plaques add so much to the personality of London that one wonders why there are not more of them. Martin Hall, however, explains that inifinite care and research are required to make sure that every plaque really deserves its place. The process of enquiry reminds me of the canonisation of a saint or choice of a pope. It sometimes takes years of argument before the 'white smoke' goes up from an office in Whitehall or Westminster. Meanwhile we must be thankful for the names which have made the grade, and to Martin Hall for his 'peep behind the plaques'.

Elizabeth Longford

INTRODUCTION

In April 1865 an anonymous letter appeared in *The Journal of the Royal Society of Arts* suggesting a scheme to commemorate the houses in London where the famous have lived, by some form of memorial or wall tablet. The idea was well-received by the Royal Society and within a short time a Committee was established to consider the matter further. Two years later, London's first blue and circular plaque was erected on a house in Holles Street in Westminster where Lord Byron was born. In the space of the next 20 years, the Royal Society of Arts erected as many as 30 further commemorative plaques. Not all of them were blue, and not all of them were round. Some were rectangular stone tablets. Others retained the same circular shape, but were made of chocolate brown terracotta. One or two even of this period were squarish and made of bronze. In short, the methods of construction were never uniform.

The scheme, however, was a success. Visitors to London and Londoners themselves appreciated the information that appeared on the plaques. London, anyway, has always been both conscious and proud of its history, and its commemorative plaques were a pleasing way of reminding the citizens of their past, personalities and events, without being obtrusive.

The scheme today is administered by the Greater London Council and, specifically, by its able and well-informed Historic Buildings Division. The change came about shortly after the formation of what was then the London County Council in 1888. The Council was prepared to adopt a similar scheme to the one administered by the Royal Society of Arts and, when it was suggested that the Council should take it over, the matter was quickly and amicably agreed.

Today, there are well over 350 commemorative plaques in the Greater London area and most of them are the familiar blue ones referred to in the title of this book. By far the most pleasing aspect of this whole scheme is that anybody is free to suggest to the Greater London Council's Historic Buildings Division that a house or a building is worthy of commemoration, through its association with a famous name from the past.

The scheme is therefore London's and, indeed, the Nation's way of honouring the great, and of saying a posthumous 'thank you' to them for enhancing and enriching people's lives through their achievements. Suggestions for Blue Plaques come, in the main, from groups of people rather than individuals. On receipt of the inquiry, a careful and thorough procedure is set into motion by the Greater London Council's Historic Buildings Division. Two primary factors are considered at this stage. First, did the subject, in fact, live or stay for a specific length of time at the address in question and, secondly, is he or she worthy of commemoration? In other words, is the subject's legacy to mankind of lasting and important significance in their particular field? The building, too, is an important consideration. If it has changed enormously since the subject lived there, then this factor will lessen the chances of a Blue Plaque eventually being granted. After all these researches are complete, the final evidence is placed before a selected committee of distinguished men and women for their final vote of whether or not the plaque should be erected.

The plaques themselves are manufactured by a number of firms with Carters of Poole, the leading specialists. Doultons and Delph are two other names associated with their manufacture. Once the design and inscription has been chosen, the plaque is then made, using kaolin-feldspathic clay. This is in order that it shall be frost-proof, an important factor for an object whose outdoor life expectancy is every bit as long as the person it is commemorating. When all this is finished, and the Blue Plaque firmly fixed to the wall of the house in question, a simple unveiling ceremony takes place on the pavement outside, attended by local dignitaries, representatives of the group from which the initial suggestion for the plaque came, and from time to time members of the family of the person being commemorated.

When this book was first being planned it was difficult to decide whether to approach the subject of the Blue Plaques of London as a gazetteer and write equal portions of text about each single plaque or whether, instead, to treat the book itself rather like a meander through some of London's historic streets, pausing when a name of some unusual interest occurs and passing by some of the others, simply only taking note of the site where they are situated. Finally, the decision was made not to attempt the gazetteer book approach. Not only is such a format both limiting and repetitive after a time, but with so much colourful information to write about, and so many little known anecdotes to include about the famous men and women who lived in London, there was neither time nor room to spend telling people how to get to the different plaques and what to look for once they arrive. The assumption is that people, and even foreign visitors, who don't know London, are capable of finding their way to certain addresses by the simple precaution of arming themselves with a street guide. Every address of the plaques in London is given in the text, complete with postal district reference letters.

The book has been arranged in three broad areas. The largest section deals with Central London and the remaining two parts cover North and South London, where only a rela-

tively few plaques are to be found. Sometimes the more obvious names of history are dealt with sparingly. This can be for a number of reasons. At times it is because the subject achieved his or her greatness abroad or that there is really very little of interest recorded about them that relates to their life in the house where they are commemorated, or its vicinity in London. Finally, it is because some of the less well-known names do provide us with a great deal of amusement and insight through their various activities and the stories they left behind them. But, most important of all, the book aims to be entertaining, lively and informative reading, as well as a service for the more energetic who may now wish to stroll through some of London's streets in search of the houses where the famous Blue Plaques commemorate those who lived there.

CENTRA

LONDON

CHELSEA

'Then Chelsea begins, rare old Chelsea', wrote Sydney Jones in his justly celebrated book, *Thames Triumphant*. 'Chelsea, full of beauty mixed with the commonplace, rich in past associations both good and otherwise.' Indeed, Chelsea has attracted interest for hundreds of years. Sir Thomas More's house stood in the midst of rich pastures and trees overlooking the river where the Embankment now runs. Later the same land was bought by **Sir Hans Sloane** (1660–1753) the famous physician and naturalist, and President of The Royal Society commemorated by a plaque at **King's Mead, King's Road, SW1**. He bequeathed some land to the Parish of Chelsea, and lent his name to Sloane Street, and Sloane Square, prettiest and most continental of London's meeting places. Chelsea was renowned for its air, and ailing bankers and merchants from the City made it their home, bringing to it an elegance and air of munificence that can still be seen today.

In the nineteenth century Chelsea was a renowned market gardening centre, and where the King's Road now stands there was then, in blossom time, an area ablaze with flowers, young fruit and vegetables destined for distant Covent Garden. Its romance has not faded. Even today its gardens are amongst the finest kept in London, and there is an air of refinement and relaxation in its streets, squares and alleyways, as well as a river frontage of magnificent character. In years gone by it was not surprising that artists and writers should have been attracted by its freedom, a focal point being Cheyne Walk, and the criss-cross pattern of old Chelsea streets between the Thames and the King's Road, with Battersea and Albert Bridge leading to it.

Cheyne Walk is now a busy thoroughfare, but in the mid-nineteenth century it was a quiet and narrow riverside trackway. The houses bordering the waterfront have housed many notable men and women, as the plaques there show.

In **Lindsey House, 98 Cheyne Walk, SW3** lived **Marc Brunel** and his son Isambard, whose names are as renowned in the history of inventions as their creations themselves. They lived in this house from 1808 to 1824, see-sawing between fame and misfortune. Lindsey House, now owned by the National Trust, was built in 1674 on the site of Sir Thomas More's farm. In the eighteenth century it became the headquarters of the Moravian brethren, a Czech religious brotherhood, who had considerable influence on the English Methodists. It is a large house, bold in stature. Brunel senior, a Frenchman, had come to England after fleeing the 1789 Revolution. He was an avowed Royalist, and was soon working for the British government against Napoleon designing machines for producing ship blocks. Later, he devoted his interests to experimenting with steamboats on the river Thames, but when a saw-mill in Battersea burnt down in 1821, and he lost the means of producing the specially bent timber for these boats, his business collapsed. He was bankrupted and thrown into prison for debt. It was only through the generosity of his old Admiralty friends, who remembered his service to the nation during the Napoleonic menace, that he regained his liberty, as well as a government grant of £5,000. It was this financial rehabilitation which allowed him, in 1824, to form the company which, nearly twenty years later, completed his scheme for boring the first tunnel under the Thames between Rotherhithe and Wapping. For much of this time his son Isambard was working with him, and though, in London at any rate, Isambard is chiefly remembered for his associations with the Great Western Rail-

Isambard Kingdom Brunel standing in front of the 'Great Eastern' at her launching in 1858, in Poplar. The 'Great Eastern' was one of the largest vessels ever to be launched on the Thames. Some idea of her size can be imagined from the strength of the chain links needed to stabilise her in the tidal waters before she was capable of producing her own power.

way, it was once more on the river Thames that he executed the most romantic feat of his long and enterprising career. This was the building of the mighty *Great Eastern*, the largest steamship of the century, in one of the last remaining London shipyards in Poplar. So large was she, 693 feet in length, that Brunel had to build her broadside onto the river. Alas, the *Great Eastern* proved to be little more than an expensive, and a very costly daydream. After less than thirty outings she was declared unmanageable by those who had to sail in her. Isambard died in 1859, the year following her launch.

The influence of water, and of the Thames in particular, is marked too in the career of **James Whistler** (1834–1903) the American painter, who is commemorated by a plaque next door at **96 Cheyne Walk, SW3**. Whistler, a proud man, with a powerful, arresting personality, became a legend in his lifetime, courting the Bohemian image that is popularly associated with Chelsea. Sporting a broad-rimmed hat, monocle and a flowing velvet coat, he strolled these streets with the largesse of a circus ringmaster, leaving in his trail a small army of cowering fellow artists, whip-lashed into silence by the sharpness of his tongue. A genuinely creative artist, who is justly accredited as one of the first true Impressionists, Whistler despised the more whimsical embroidery of so many painters then attracting more critical attention in London than he was.

At this house in Cheyne Walk, he worked in a second floor studio overlooking the rear gardens. Time, when he worked, meant nothing to him. One of his sitters, Thomas Carlyle, became so restless and irritable at the mealtimes he missed it is a wonder his portrait was ever finished at all. One day, after a lengthy, tedious sitting, Carlyle was leaving the house to find a young girl sitting on the doorstep. On learning this eight-year-old was to be Whistler's next victim that day, Carlyle shook

Below: *This satirical drawing of Whistler by Spy from an issue of 'Vanity Fair' in 1878 neatly catches the American painter's self proclaimed arrogance. Whistler was one of the first painters to attain truly Bohemian status in London towards the closing years of the nineteenth century.*
Right: *These houses in Cheyne Walk provide a magnificent river frontage to the River Thames. Set in the heart of historic old Chelsea, these residences abound with memories of the famous writers and painters who have lived there.*

his grey head sadly, murmuring in his soft Scottish accent, 'Puir Lassie . . . . . puir lassie!' The girls, Ciciley Alexander, was the daughter of one of Whistler's much needed patrons, and was the subject of his celebrated 'Arrangement in Grey and Green'.

Walter Greaves (1855–1897) who lived a few doors away at **104 Cheyne Walk, SW3**, is a name for ever linked with Whistler, and the story of their relationship is poignant, savage and rare. Greaves's father ran a Thames boatyard, ferrying goods and people about the river. Walter and his brother were two of the ferrymen. They were cocky characters, bright and cheerful opportunists. Whistler met them soon after he had moved to Chelsea, and whenever he needed transportation on the river, it was their taxi service that he used. The brothers, and Walter in particular, were both fascinated and impressed by their famous client, and assumed an unofficial apprenticeship with him, helping in his studio, and mixing with his guests at his parties. Walter had a good eye and a straight brush and was very soon showing that he could also paint. Whistler was amused by his young pupil, and if Walter's paintings were a little derivative of his own this was hardly surprising. Whistler, after all, was the supreme egoist. On their walks along the leafy embankment, or cruising beneath the wooden uprights of Old Battersea Bridge, Walter would have seen everything, every shade of light, and each delicate nuance of colour, through Whistler's eyes. But when, in later years, Greaves was still imitating and copying Whistler in almost everything that he painted, and even, in some cases, claiming the originality of the canvasses, the relationship soured into open nastiness. Greaves outlived his mentor by nearly thirty years, and photographs taken towards the end of his life show him a sad, dandyish figure, still possessed of the airs of importance that once infatuated him, and still boasting the triumphs that were never really his.

Hilaire Belloc the writer and historian also lived at this house at 104 Cheyne Walk for nearly five years at the turn of the century.

Two lady novelists are commemorated in Cheyne Walk, but both had only the briefest of associations with their respective houses. George Eliot (1819–1880) died at 4 Cheyne Walk, SW3 in December 1880, after living in the house for only three weeks. (See also page 140 for main entry in Wandsworth) Mrs Gaskell (1810–1865) was born at 93 Cheyne Walk, but as her mother died shortly after her birth she moved shortly afterwards to be looked after by an aunt in Knutsford in Cheshire, the Cranford of Mrs Gaskell's most celebrated book.

Thomas Carlyle's stay in Chelsea was not so brief. 'Our row runs out upon a parade running along the shore of the river'. Thomas Carlyle (1795–1881) wrote enthusiastically to his wife after discovering the house at 24 Cheyne Row, SW3, and deciding to buy it: '. . . a broad highway with huge shady trees, boats lying moored and a smell of shipping and tar. Battersea Bridge is a few yards off; the broad river with white-trousered, white-shirted Cockneys dashing about like arrows in their long canoes of boats and beyond the green beautiful knolls of Surrey with their villages.' The house is now a wonderfully preserved museum in memory of one of the greatest writers in the English language, but only a few years after Carlyle's death it was, according to a contemporary report, 'untenanted, and neglected; its windows were unwashed, a pane of glass was broken; its threshold appeared untrodden, its whole aspect forlorn and desolate'. Such reports motivated a group of the great historian's admirers to buy the house for its present use. It is now managed by the National Trust.

Carlyle was 39 when he came to live in Chelsea, and he liked it from the start. It was a 'genteel neighbourhood, two ladies on one side, unknown character on the other, but with "pianos" '. Leigh Hunt lived nearby and Car-lyle used to visit him often. One of the treasures of the house was its garden which, Carlyle wrote to his mother, 'is of admirable comfort to me in the smoking way. I can wander about in a dressing gown and straw hat, and take my pipe in peace'. A photograph of the time shows the contented householder sitting in an upright chair doing just that, though whether he is listening to a melody from the 'unknown character' is not recorded. Certainly Carlyle was anything but contented one evening in Cheyne Row when his friend, John Stuart Mill called on him. Carlyle had lent him the manuscript of the first volume of his essay *The French Revolution*. The manuscript had just been completed after many months of painstaking work, but all that remained of it that evening was its charred remains. One of Stuart Mill's servants had been using it to light a fire in an upstairs bedroom. Carlyle looked, according to Mill, 'as pale as Hector's ghost' on hearing what had happened.

Leigh Hunt, the essayist and novelist, is commemorated at 22 Upper Cheyne Row, SW3. Hunt, while he lived here, was a struggling writer of middle years with a large family to feed. During his time here Hunt wrote *The Indicator; The London Journal* and *Captain Short and Captain Pen*. Curiously, though, Hunt's only mention of Chelsea in his writings comes in his autobiography, despite a stay there of nearly seven years. Some years later, after moving to Edwardes Square in Kensington, he was to write in a letter to Douglas Jerrold: 'It will do your kindly eyes good to see the nice study into which I have escaped out of the squalidities of Chelsea.' In his autobiography, however, he wrote of his stay in Upper Cheyne Row: 'My family moved to a corner in Chelsea where the air was so refreshing, and the quiet of the thoroughfares so full of repose, that although our fortunes were at their worst, and my health almost a piece of them, I felt for some weeks as if I could sit for ever, embalmed

Leigh Hunt's house in Upper Cheyne Row, Chelsea, is only a few minutes' stroll away from the equally modest one where his friend, the great historian Thomas Carlyle had his residence. The two men used to stroll through these quiet Chelsea Streets to visit one another. Leigh Hunt's house is now a private residence, but Carlyle's House is now a museum, open to the public, administered by the National Trust.

in the silence.' The discrepancy between the two descriptions is intriguing, though perhaps the earlier allusion is to a noisy household full of ill-disciplined children, ignorant of their father's need to work, rather than the area itself.

A plaque nearby in **Lawrence Street, SW3** commemorating the site of the famous Chelsea China factory also recalls a pleasing mystery about this area of Chelsea. Certainly, there was a China factory here between 1750 and 1762, but the exact site has been lost. From time to time different fragments of porcelain found in local gardens provide the enthusiasts and experts with new information, but the truth is no one knows exactly where the factory stood. Dr Johnson would have known, however, for he tried his hand at making pottery down at the Lawrence Street factory, surrounded by the great craftsmen from Venice and Dresden. But no matter how hard Johnson tried to turn a good pot he failed. Accompanied on his expeditions to Chelsea by his housekeeper, whose task it was to keep him amply provided with food from a large hamper, the Doctor had access to all parts of the factory except the mixing room, whose secrets even so celebrated a person as he was not allowed to share. There is a fine collection of Chelsea China at the Victoria and Albert Museum, but it does not contain any pieces made by Johnson. None of his compositions withstood the fiercesome heat of the ovens, and the Doctor wisely abandoned his sortie into the world of handicrafts, probably much to the relief of his poor housekeeper.

This same plaque in Lawrence Street, also commemorates **Tobias Smollett** (1721–1771), the novelist, who lived across the road in lovely, creaking Monmouth House. The art of ceramics is commemorated too by the plaque to **William de Morgan** (1839–1917), ceramic artist and novelist, and to his wife Evelyn, who lived at **127 Old Church Street, SW3**. William de Morgan was

The austerity and dignity of this exterior to Oscar Wilde's house in Tite Street, Chelsea, reveals little of the flamboyant lifestyle of the author within.

an original, 'recreating' as the memorial tablet in Old Chelsea Church puts it, 'in ceramic work, upon his own vigorous designs, the colour of the Persian and the lustre of the great Umbrian craftsmen'. A friend of William Morris, de Morgan created the most brilliant effects in his ceramics, rediscovering and enhancing the techniques of the lost world. He was an idealist, though, settling for nothing less than perfection in his work, and since the production of his tiles and plates, often to designs by his wife, rarely matched the magnificence of his original vision, he frequently felt he was failing his very high artistic ideals. It was just such a failure that provoked him one day to destroy all his notebooks in which he had laboriously documented all the secrets of his craft. That he was then able, so late in life, to begin as a novelist, at an age when Dickens, Balzac, Fielding and Zola were all dead, is a mark of his versatility. His novels were by no means so memorable, or creative, as his former work, nevertheless he was, as his memorial proclaims 'beloved by all who knew the breadth of his intellectual interest, his catholic sympathy, genial humour and lambent wit'.

When **Oscar Wilde** married in 1883, and needed a house for his bride, it was to **34 Tite Street, SW3** that he moved. Oscar Wilde was then just at the beginning of his dazzling career. He did his writing, Hesketh Pearson recounts in his biography of Wilde, 'in a small room downstairs facing the street on a table which had once been Carlyle's and which he hoped would be an incentive to work'. Whistler helped decorate this house, even presenting some of his Venetian studies for the rooms upstairs. He was a friend of Wilde's, though there is some truth in the suggestion that it was more jealousy of Wilde's wit than actual friendship that occasioned their acquaintanceship. Wilde enjoyed himself in Chelsea at this time. He would be seen frequently striding along the King's Road towards Oakley Street where his mother

lived, to her frequent soirées, to meet, amongst others, his drunkard journalist brother whom Wilde admonished for taking yet another 'alcoholiday' away from his work.

By the time Wilde's fame was at its zenith in the 1890s, Pearson tells us 'he could no longer find time to attend his mother's functions, so the celebrities disappeared from Oakley Street and the crowds began to dwindle'.

George Alexander, who is commemorated at **57 Pont Street, SW1** and **Herbert Beerbohm Tree**, commemorated at **76 Sloane Street, SW1** were two London theatrical managers who prospered from Wilde's dramatic genius. Wilde's first play, which he described as 'one of those modern drawing room plays with pink lampshades', was *Lady Windermere's Fan*. It opened in February 1892 and was an immediate success. Two years later *A Woman Of No Importance* Opened for Tree at the Haymarket Theatre, followed in 1895 by *The Importance of Being Earnest*, written in an astonishing three weeks when Wilde was holidaying with his wife and two sons the previous summer in Worthing. Wilde, at this time, was one of the most glittering personalities in London. But not for long. The gossip in London's clubs and salons was all about Wilde's homosexuality, and it was not difficult to foresee his downfall when fully exposed to the vicious loathing which was the Victorian attitude to anything overtly sexual. Wilde's eventual trial and imprisonment formed a lurid and melancholy final act to an otherwise glittering life.

Arnold Bennett (1867–1931) the novelist, commemorated at **75 Cadogan Square, SW1**, who was only a young man in his early twenties at the time of Wilde's downfall, lived a life that was almost austere by contrast. He came to live here shortly after the First World War by which time he had passed the most celebrated passage of his career. Frank Swinnerton in his *Bookman's London* recalls Bennett's house here: 'His pictures were modern; his drawing room glittered and was comfortless, but the drawing room, entirely Victorian, was irresistible. When I first visited this house I objected brusquely to the whim of some previous occupant who had pannelled every door with mirrors. I said "I couldn't stand all this looking glass!" Bennett, the least vain of men, replied blandly, "I . . . was born for it!" '

FURTHER NAMES COMMEMORATED IN CHELSEA

Other plaques in Chelsea have been struck to the memory of **Astafieva**, at **152 King's Road, SW3**, one of Diaghilev's ballet dancers, and herself a great teacher; and to **Graham Wallas** (1858–1932) at **38 St Leonard's Terrace, SW3**, opposite the Royal Chelsea Hospital. Wallas, a political psychologist, was involved in the founding of the London School of Economics, where he later became Professor of Political Science. **George Gissing** (1857–1903) the novelist, is commemorated on the wall of **33 Oakley Gardens, SW3**, where he lived as a young man. **Mark Twain** (1835–1910) is remembered for his two year stay at **23 Tedworth Square, SW3** which runs on from St Leonard's Terrace, and where he lived 1896–97. **George Rippon** (1827–1909) Viceroy of India, is recalled on the walls of **9 Chelsea Embankment, SW3**. **Dante Gabriel Rossetti** (1828–1882) one of Chelsea's most flamboyant figures, is commemorated at **16 Cheyne Walk, SW3** but his childhood and later close association with Charles Swinburne are described on pages 85 and 137. **John F. Sartorius** (1775–1830) the sporting painter, lived at **155 Old Church Street, SW3**. **Philip Steer** (1860–1942) the painter, lived at **109 Cheyne Walk, SW3**. **Richard Cobden** (1804–1865) statesman, died at **23 Suffolk Street, W1**.

Although the original north side of Tedworth Square in Chelsea has now been demolished, the house where Samuel Langhorne Clemens, alias 'Mark Twain' stayed, still survives.

KENSINGTON

The sale of a modest mansion standing in sloping fields marked the beginning of Kensington as one of London's premier boroughs. The purchaser of the house was William III, who, anxious for an alternative residence away from Whitehall and the unpleasant Thameside mists that so upset his asthma, gave the job of transforming it into a royal palace to Sir Christopher Wren. Kensington was chosen as a royal resort because of the air from some nearby gravel pits at Notting Hill Gate, which was said to contain wonderful healing powers. The gravel pits stood in a not very clearly defined area both north and south of the Bayswater Road. 'It is just as probable', declared Samuel Garth in his book of 1719 called *Dispensary,* 'that the Alps would sink to vales as that the rich would change the gravel pits for the Kentish air!' It was not until the reign of Queen Anne that Kensington Palace was used almost permanently by the monarch. Then, because the court had settled there, there was a rapid scramble for accommodation as Ambassadors and foreign notables sought residences close to the palace. The beginning of Kensington's development stems from this time.

William Thackeray, who is commemorated at **2 Palace Gardens, W8**, identified closely with this period. Though living a hundred years later, and though he was a superb commentator on life in the nineteenth century, it was with the court of Queen Anne that his interest lay. There are three plaques in Kensington to commemorate Thackeray's life in the borough. The first is at **16 Young Street, W8**, which leads into Kensington Square. Thackeray exclaimed, on seeing the house for the first time, 'it has the air of a feudal castle. I'll have a

flagstaff put over the coping of the wall and hoist a standard when I'm at home!'. Certainly this lovely grey brick house is worth celebrating for it was here Thackeray wrote *Vanity Fair.* While living here, he took frequent walks to nearby Kensington Gardens, revelling in the proximity of Kensington Palace, and forming in his mind the shape of a biography of Queen Anne he wished someday to write.

In 1853 Thackeray moved to **36 Onslow Square, SW7**, site of the second plaque. 'A shabby, genteel house', he called it. One of Thackeray's daughters wrote of it later: 'Our old home was the fourth, counting the end house, from the corner by the church in Onslow Square, the church being on the left hand, and the avenue of trees running in front of our drawing room windows. I used to look up from the avenue and see my father's head bending over his work in the study window, which was over the drawing room. There he would work all morning dressed in dressing gown and slippers and smoking a cigar which was constantly going out.' While at Onslow Gardens Thackeray wrote *The Newcomes, The Virginians,* his lectures on the four Georges, and *The Rose and The Ring.* In addition to all this he was writing for *Punch,* about to stand for Parliament, undertake his second American lecture tour, and become editor of the *Cornhill* magazine. Luckily for him, the first editions of the *Cornhill* quickly showed that he had a success on his hands, and when he heard that the house at **2 Palace Gardens, W8** was about to become vacant, he quickly began negotiations.

The Green, anciently called The Moor, was the site of the Palace's kitchen gardens, and No. 2 was for some years the residence of the Royal Ranger. During the middle years of the nineteenth century, the house had fallen more and more into disrepair. On looking over the house, Thackeray realised that if he was to live there, so close to his beloved Kensington Palace, he would have to rebuild. He then

Below: *This manuscript is a portion of 'Denis Duval',*
Thackeray's last work, which remained unfinished at
the time of his death. Thackeray himself drew the
sketch in the margin.
Left: *Thackeray's house at 2 Palace Green, was designed*
from an original sketch by Thackeray himself.
Standing within sight of Thackeray's beloved
Kensington Palace, it is built on the site of Palace's old
kitchen gardens.
Right: *A sketch of Thackeray by Richard Doyle.*

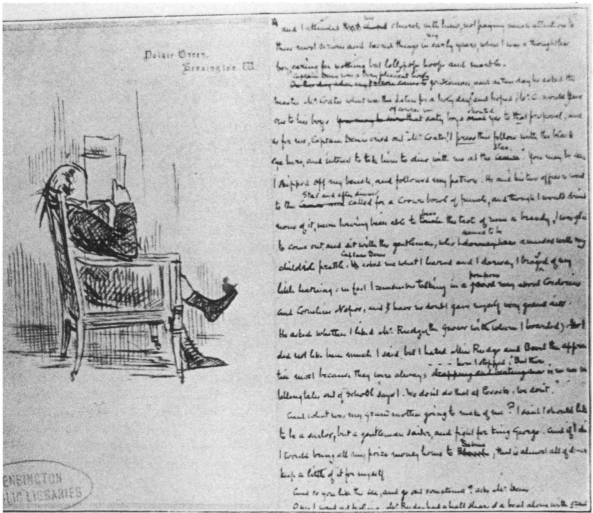

A PAGE OF THACKERAY'S MANUSCRIPT.

Specially photographed for THE BOOKMAN.

manuscript is a portion of " Denis Duval," Thackeray's last work, which remained unfinished at his dea
margin is one of his own sketches, which is now published for the first time.

(Reproduced by kind permission of Mrs. Richmond Ritchie.)

Right: *John Stuart Mill in his middle years.*
Far right: *The spacious gardens of Kensington Square, W8, one of London's noblest surviving developments from the late eighteenth century, looking across to Sir Charles Hubert Parry's residence at No. 17. Next door, at No. 18, John Stuart Mill lived.*

committed himself to design a house after his own heart. It was a costly business. Initially the building budget was £4,000. Within months it had risen to £5,200, but by the time it was finished, and Thackeray and his daughter had moved in, the total cost of the house had escalated to over £8,000, a princely sum in those days. 'My dear relatives', he wrote to some friends in America, 'are furious at my arrogance and extravagance and presumption in building so handsome a new house. If I live, please God, I shall write the history of Queen Anne there in that room with the arched window which had a jolly look out on the noble Kensington Gardens elms.' Alas, Thackeray's optimism was not to be, for only months later, on Christmas Eve 1863, he died suddenly in his sleep. 'He was found', wrote his friend Dickens, 'peacefully lying, undisturbed, and to all appearances asleep. He was only in his fifty-third year; so young a man that the mother who blessed him in his first sleep blessed him also at his last.'

Most eminent of those who are commemorated by a plaque in Kensington Square is **John Stuart Mill**, the philosopher and reformer, who lived at **18 Kensington Square, W8**. Mill (1806–1879), who wrote to convince not merely expound, produced both his *System of Logic* and the *Principles of Political Economy* while living in this house. Mill lived here from 1837 to 1851 with his mother and sister, only leaving on his marriage to Mrs Taylor. A sketch of *A System of Logic* had first been written in 1832, but it was not until 1837 that he seriously applied himself to the task of the book, completing it four years later. It was eventually published in 1843, having suffered a rebuff from the first publisher to whom Mill has offered it. After finishing *Logic* he was exhausted. He declared at dinner one night that he entertained serious hopes of an illness that winter, but was conscientious enough not to encourage it!

It is from Caroline Fox's Diary that we get the following glimpse of John Stuart Mill at home. The entry is dated May 19 1840, and she and Harriet Mill had been to attend one of Carlyle's lectures, this time on *Heroes*. 'After it was over,' she records, 'we returned to their house in Kensington Square where we were most lovingly received by all the family. After dinner we walked in the little garden, and saw portions of John Mill's immense herbarium, being finally shown his charming library, the mother so anxious to show everything, and her son so terribly afraid of boring us.' That Mill was a conscientious host is also detailed by his remark just as his guests were sitting down to eat. 'No-one', beamed Mill, flicking his serviette across his lap, 'need feel any delicacy in canvassing his opinions in my presence!' Whether this was merely intellectual humility on his part, or a tacit invitation to a good argument about Carlyle's lecture is not recorded! Caroline Fox's Diary ends by noting that 'Jeremy Bentham's favourite pudding was served at supper'. Bentham, who had been a great friend of the family, and particularly of Mill's father, had died as long ago as eight years before, and it is touching to think that Mill's mother still instructed the cook to prepare dishes that brought back associations of the great writer with her husband. Happy the cook may have been in her work, but history does not record what terrible words Mill himself must have uttered when, one raw March morning in 1832, he made the appalling discovery of the burnt manuscript, (see page 17).

Next door, at **17 Kensington Square, W8**, lived **Sir Charles Parry** who displayed so many varied talents in his chosen work that he is more aptly remembered as a musician rather than just as a composer. Influenced by Wagner whom he met in London in 1876, his composition began the real revival in English contemporary music. Writer of books, composer, and Professor of Music at the newly founded Royal College of Music, and later at Oxford as well, Parry,

Left: Holman Hunt photographed in later years.
Below: The large room on the ground floor in Sir Charles Stanford's house in Holland Street, Kensington, is where many musical soirées were held during the composer's 22 years of residence at this address. Further along at 13 Holland Street is the handsome, gaunt mansion where **Walter Crane** *(1845–1915), the artist and engraver lived.*

through his enthusiasm, personal standing, and widespread professional capabilities, effected a much needed improvement in the social and intellectual status of music and musicians in Victorian England. He took up residence here in 1886, and occupied the house during his time at the Royal College of Music, where he shared the chair with **Sir Charles Stanford**, whose house at **56 Hornton Street, W8**, only a short walk away, is also commemorated.

Finally, at **40 Kensington Square, W8**, there is a plaque to the memory of **Sir John Simon**, the pioneer of public health. After a training in surgery at St Thomas's Hospital, Simon was appointed Medical Officer of Health for The City of London in 1848. It was only the second such appointment in the whole of Britain, and at that time cholera outbreaks were all too commonplace and Simon had a massive task ahead of him to persuade central government that only stringent legislation could prevent similar outbreaks in the future. But his ideas and schemes for the guarantee of good public health were expensive, and this led to a long drawn out conflict with the Treasury. Simon was a man of wide literary and artistic tastes. Through Ruskin, with whom he enjoyed a strong friendship, a distinguished group of people began coming to his house. Holman Hunt, William Morris and Edward Burne-Jones, who himself also lived in Kensington Square for two years, all visited him. In later years Simon was remembered as a quaint, little figure, wearing a long circular cape of black cloth and a flat brimmed, high hat, even then out of fashion, walking daily through the Square. 'It was an attractive sight', goes a contemporary report, 'to see him surrounded by a bevy of his very young neighbours, two of Thackeray's grandchildren amongst them, walking up Young Street, past the house where *Vanity Fair* was written, en route for Herbert and Jones where he placed his small friends at the little marble topped tables and provided

them with ices. From inside his pocket he would produce a book of verse and commence to read from it.'

The mention of Sir John Simon is a timely reminder of the abject and dreadful social conditions suffered by the majority of Londoners at this time. That the public health is now a priority for any central or local government administration is in no small way due to the work of Sir John Simon.

Grandeur, however, and generous helpings of it, was the astonishing lifestyle of **Lord Frederick Leighton**, whose house in Holland Park was the focal point of the pre-Raphaelite colony that settled in this area after 1860.

Thackeray, Leighton, Tennyson, G. F. Watts the portrait painter, Rossetti, Burne-Jones, Macaulay, Coleridge and Mrs Cameron, taking her photographs on the lawns, and even Gladstone and Disraeli were all visitors here, Leighton, a wealthy man, decided to build a house which embodied all the extravagant aestheticism of his age. He chose for **Leighton House** a site in Holland Park Road which was, at that time, no more than a narrow lane of small cottages, trees and stables.

Leighton House was completed in 1866. Its most memorable feature is the Arab Hall, its dome decorated with fourteenth, fifteenth and seventeenth century tiles collected by Leighton on his trips to the Middle East with his friend Sir Richard Burton, translator of *The Arabian Nights*.

Frequent visitors to Leighton Hall were the members of the pre-Raphaelite group of artists who lived in the immediate area. G. F. Watts, who was at that time living in Melbury Road, came almost daily. His whirlwind marriage to **Ellen Terry** (commemorated at **22 Barkston Gardens, SW7**, where she lived briefly) was now over, and he had resumed his portrait painting. Other members of the group were **Holman-Hunt**, living at **18 Melbury Road, W14**, and **Luke Filde**, the painter and **Hamo Thorneycroft**, the sculptor, living at

Nos. 31 and 2 Melbury Road, W14 respectively. **Sir Edward Elgar** (1867–1934) composer lived at **51 Avonmore Road, W14**.

Henry James (see page 34), who was a guest at Leighton's famous Sunday receptions wrote: 'Leighton in particular overwhelms me – his sumptuosity, his personal beauty, his cleverness, his gorgeous house, his universal attainments, his portraits of Duchesses, his universal parties, his perfect French and Italian – and German – his general air of being above all human dangers and difficulties!' James, had he known Leighton better, might also have mentioned his legendary generosity. His kindness to others in need, and especially his fellow artists, was sometimes embarassing. The story goes that William de Morgan, in striving to perfect the amazing peacock blue tiles that can be seen on the stairs, far overspent on his original estimate for the job, but still avoided telling Leighton of his extra expenses for fear of what Leighton might do to redress the balance. Curiously, though, for all his munificence, Leighton himself was a frugal man. He enjoyed good company, and provided well for it, and to none more than those who shared his own creative tastes. To the world of commerce he was suspicious and guarded. Unlike his friend Millais, he was stern and uncompromising to agents, dealers and those who pandered, as he saw it, to public taste. Art, and the high ideals that motivated it, were all to Leighton. It was a spirit in keeping with the age, and one which brought Leighton friendship. President of The Royal Academy he died in 1896.

'Death, in striking him down', trumpetted an obituary in 1896 with all the gothic pomposity the writer could summon from his pen, 'has struck a heavy blow at English art – a fact which it is well nigh impossible to exaggerate!' The lamented subject of this journalistic wreath was not Leighton, but Millais, who died in the same year.

Sir John Everett Millais (1826–1896), whose house

Right: *The sheer size and munificence of Luke Filde's mansion in Melbury Road, Kensington, reflects the enormous incomes earned by successful painters in the middle years of the nineteenth century. Filde's home had over 40 rooms, and was decorated everywhere with extravagant features. Even the weathervane includes the painter's initials in its tail.*

Below: *Leighton House, once the home of Lord Leighton, the painter, is now a museum and gallery managed by the Royal Borough of Kensington and Chelsea. The superb interiors are open to inspection by members of the public, and contain many fascinating associations with Leighton and the other foremost artists of his day. This photograph shows the exterior of the famous Arab dome.*

at 2 **Palace Gate, W8** is also commemorated by a plaque, was established as one of the foremost artists of his day by the time work began on the building of this mansion in 1873. Also by this time, Millais, through his commissions to paint many society figures and their children, was earning as much as £30,000 in a single year. Though he had been a founder member of the pre-Raphaelite movement together with Holman Hunt and Rossetti, his style had long since evolved away from such high minded purism into something much more commercial. But since he was only 19 when he had made this original creative pact this is hardly surprising. Besides, Millais was a creature of comfort. He loved to shoot and fish, and enjoyed special Royal permission to fish the Serpentine in nearby Hyde Park. He was also especially fond of Scotland. He frequently painted dressed in slippers and an old shooting coat, with a pipe jammed in his mouth. It was as a result of a holiday to Scotland with John Ruskin and his wife, that a relationship was formed with Mrs Ruskin. When, in 1854, her marriage to Ruskin was annulled on the grounds of the critic's impotence, Millais had no further unease about his attractions towards her. They were married a year later, and soon had a fine family of four children. Two of these appeared in Millais's famous 'The Boyhood of Raleigh', while a grandchild, Willie, was the subject for 'Bubbles', the world famous work that was the first serious painting ever to be used in a commercial advertisement.

The house at 2 Palace Gate, which stands to the south of Kensington Gardens, and a stone's throw away from the Royal Albert Hall, is one of the best known and most extensively documented Victorian mansions in London. Its layout and construction incorporated many unusual features specified by Millais himself. John Oldcastle, writing in 1881, stated: 'Mr Millais has built himself a house into which the aestheticism of the day does not enter; no, not

Top left: *Sir John Millais' house at 2 Palace Gate, SW7.*
Left: *A drawing of Sir John Millais in 'Vanity Fair',*
May 13 1871.
Below: *Sir John Millais is shown here photographed in*
his studio at 2 Palace Gate, SW7, which is commonly
recognised as one of the finest examples of Victorian
residential architecture anywhere in London. Formerly
an embassy, the mansion has now been superbly
restored by its new occupants, an international bank.

Left: *Henry James in his study at 34 De Vere Gardens, Kensington.*
Right: *An unflattering drawing of Jenny Lind which does little justice to the alluring beauty of The Swedish Nightingale, who bewitched the hearts of her admirers as much by her looks as the sweetness of her voice.*

by so much as a peacock feather.' An allusion, no doubt, to several such birds who strutted with such sinewy aplomb through the Arab Hall back at Leighton House. Walter Armstrong, writing in 1885, described Millais's house for us. 'From the sides towards the park the most conspicuous thing is the great studio window . . . the hall is a room about five and twenty foot square, with a marble pavement and dado. To the right of the hall is the dining room. On the first floor landing we find the famous fountain with [Sir Edgar] Boehm's black marble seal. The studio is about 40 feet long, 25 feet wide and 20 high. It is lit by electricity and on three of the walls hang Italian tapestries. In the left hand corner is the bureau [easel] and near it a table covered with the artist's painting materials. In the centre stands a dais for his models, and facing it, at the end of the room, is the large canvas of "Time Clipping The Wings of Love" by Vandyke.'

Another unusual feature of the studio is a long slit in the floor, communicating with the storeroom below and the large exit door to the private road, so that Millais's largest canvasses could be removed easily. 'Millais was always glad to see his friends in the half hour following breakfast', a contemporary report tells us. 'He was also very fond of music which, he said, helped him in his work. The piano stood in the drawing room separated from the studio by folding doors . . . as the hour drew near for the morning's work he would roll the partitions aside, saying, "I wouldn't say 'No' to a little music".' The portraits of Gladstone, Disraeli, Tennyson, Henry Irving and Carlyle were all painted here in this studio. It was on one of his visits that Carlyle compared the luxury of the house at Palace Gate to his own more modest dwelling in Cheyne Row. 'Has paint done all this, Mr Millais?' Carlyle asked with an austere sniff at all the wealth around him. 'It has!' replied Millais cheerfully. Carlyle's dour riposte was typical. 'Then there are more fools in

the world than I thought there were!' Millais died on August 13 1896, and was buried in St Paul's Cathedral. The plaque on this house was erected 30 years later in November 1926.

At **34 De Vere Gardens, W8**, the street running parallel to Palace Gate, **Henry James** (1843–1916) is remembered by a plaque. James took a 21-year lease on a fourth floor flat here in 1885, moving here from lodgings off Piccadilly. He lived here only intermittently, though he made a good friend in **Robert Browning** who is commemorated by a plaque opposite on the site of **22 De Vere Gardens, W8**. (See page 66.)

Another writer, **Kenneth Grahame** (1859–1932), lived in **16 Phillimore Place, W8**. He was 'a large, fair, genial, kindly, shy and generous man, with enormous insight into what children liked'. (*Dictionary of National Biography*) The story of how he came to write one of the all time classics of children's literature is a charming one. Grahame was then a man of some importance, being Secretary to the Bank of England. Such was the pressure of work one year that he was unable to accompany the family down to Littlehampton on their annual holidays. Alistair, Grahame's son, then aged eight, was at the time being treated to a series of bedtime stories which his father made up on the spot featuring such odd characters as Mr Toad, Water Rat and Mole. On hearing that the summer holiday would mean a whole month away from the breathtaking adventures of Mr Toad, Alistair firmly dug his heels in and refused to go. It was only when his father promised faithfully to forward the next instalment of the story in writing to the young rebel each day that Alistair relented. What was then written in the ensuing month became the genesis of one of the most delightful childrens' books of all time. Alas, though, the story had a tragic ending when Alistair, the Grahame's only son, was killed by a train near Oxford while an undergraduate at Christ Church. It was a sadness from which Grahame never recovered.

Right: Aubrey House a good example of one of the few remaining large country houses built in the eighteenth century when Kensington was little more than a village and country spa.

W. S. Gilbert is commemorated at **39 Harrington Gardens, SW7**. William Schwenck Gilbert was just two years old when he was stolen by brigands while travelling with his parents through Naples in 1838. Happily he was recovered, and the ransom of £25 paid off. It was a small sum to pay for someone whose talent, with Arthur Sullivan, was later to create the immortal Gilbert and Sullivan operas for the D'Oyly Carte Company.

Of those from the musical arts who are commemorated by a plaque none ever received the same public adulation as **Jenny Lind** (1820–1887), who is remembered at **189 Brompton Road, SW5**, which is the site of the cottage where she stayed on her first visits to England. 'The Swedish Nightingale' first came to London in 1847, lured by a contract of over £4000 to appear for a season at Her Majesty's Theatre in London. Though only aged 27, Jenny Lind was even then experienced enough to bargain with theatrical managements to agree to the deal only if she was supplied also with a house, a carriage and horses, and an extra £800 if she chose to travel to Italy at the end of the season for a rest. Benjamin Lumbley, the London impresario, frantically looked around for a suitable residence to clinch the deal. The search was far from easy, for Jenny Lind had also stipulated, 'I want to live where there are trees, and a cathedral'. In settling for Clairville Cottage, a charming little abode amongst the market gardens of Old Brompton, in what was then the south west corner of London, Lumbley was able to give her the trees, and if not a cathedral, at least a lovely church, St Mary's in The Boltons. Jenny Lind enjoyed the cottage enormously, and the church, which she used to attend, sometimes singing in the choir there.

The following year in 1848 Jenny Lind returned to London once more, again scoring an enormous success. Chopin heard her for the first time, describing her singing as 'infallibly pure and true'. Six years later she had married Otto Goldsmidt, a pianist, by whom she had three children, eventually settling in Wimbledon Park. She died in Malvern in 1887. 'It was the charm of her personality', writes the *Dictionary of National Biography*, 'probably quite as much as her wonderful voice, that won her a position in public esteem which no other singer has attained.'

The market gardens, the narrow thoroughfares that led past groups of houses, often bordering on open fields, presents a very pleasant, even rural prospect of developing Kensington in the middle years of the nineteenth century. Faulkner, writing a little earlier in 1820, and of the area around Campden Hill, has left us a picture it is hard even to contemplate today. 'The valley in the north', he wrote, 'is laid down with grass, and the whole of this district appears to have undergone but little alteration. Although the distance from London is scarcely three miles yet the traveller might imagine himself to be embosomed in the most sequestered parts of the country, for nothing is heard to interrupt the course of his limitations but the notes of the lark, the linnet or the nightingale.'

With its high ground, and excellent air, this part of Kensington was perfectly positioned to attain a reputation as one of London's spas. **Aubrey House**, in **Aubrey Road, W8**, that is marked by a plaque, stands on the site of Kensington Wells, and was the centre of the spa. The name Wells was derived from medicinal springs close by, the first owner being a Dr Wells and his partners. Other residents of this house, which had its origins as long ago as 1698, include **Sir Edward Lloyd; Richard first Earl Grosvenor; Lady Mary Coke**, a diarist, who has left some well documented local information through her letters and journals; **Peter and Clementia Taylor**, philanthropists, and **William Alexander**, an art lover, who came to the house in 1873. It was Alexander who became Whistler's patron,

commissioning him, amongst other works, to paint his daughter. Whistler was a frequent visitor to this lovely place, which stands amid lawns, flower beds and mulberry trees in a large walled garden. On one visit here, Whistler brought with him a fresh canvas which his patron had agreed to purchase. It was one of his famous 'Nocturnes' which for many years was to hang in the hall at Aubrey House. It is a private residence now, but there are few more rewarding walks for those studying the elegance of old London than in the narrow roads of this quarter where some of London's loveliest houses still exist.

16 Palace Gardens Terrace, W8, a short way up the Bayswater Road, is both an agreeable and handsome house to look at, but knowing more about its occupant one might imagine that passers-by, and even sometimes the neighbours, were once anything but relaxed as they strolled past this residence. The house is commemorated because **James Clerk Maxwell** lived here from 1862 until 1866. Students of experimental physics will remember the name well, for it was Maxwell, when appointed to the newly created chair in that science at Cambridge University in 1871, who arranged the details of the new Cavendish Physical Laboratory which opened in 1874. 'His ideas', it was written of him in the press at the time of the erection of this plaque in 1923, 'as the mathematical interpreter and continuator of Faraday, rank as the greatest advance in our understanding of the laws of the physical universe that has happened since the time of Newton.'

During his four years' residence in this house Maxwell conducted many experiments in a large garret which ran the whole length of the house. These experiments were carried out in the morning, and in the afternoon, when he was free from his duties as Professor of Natural Philosophy at King's College, London, he would ride in nearby Kensington Park. The theory of electricity and magnetism was to be the chief work in his life. Passers-by would be surprised to see him standing at an upstairs open window staring at a long black box, nearly eight feet in length, conducting his experiments. It is hardly surprising he excited the wonder of those down in the street below who thought him mad to spend so many hours staring at a coffin! Strange noises must have come from inside the garret too as he conducted yet more experiments on the viscosity of gases at different pressures and temperatures. A large fire was kept up in the room, even in the hottest of weather. 'Kettles' the same contemporary press report ran, 'were kept on the fire and large quantities of steam allowed to flow into the room. Mrs Maxwell acted as stoker, which was very exhausting work when maintained for several consecutive hours!' The five years Maxwell and his wife were to spend away on his estate at Glenair, in Kirkcudbright, after they had left this house must have seemed like heaven after the self-induced Turkish baths they had endured in the laboratory in Kensington.

One man to whom fresh air was always important is commemorated at **22 Hereford Square, SW7**. This was the philologist and scholar, **George Borrow**, who, tiring of his occupation as a publisher's hack-writer compiling the *Newgate Calendar*, and working for starvation wages, left London early one morning to go for a tramp. It was to be a long walk. Borrow travelled through England, France, Germany, Russia, Spain and in the East before returning to England, when he wrote *The Bible in Spain* in the early 1840s whilst living in Suffolk. But this sojourn in Suffolk was only a brief interlude before Borrow was off travelling again. He finally settled in Hereford Square in 1860, when he was 58, and lived here for 12 years, preoccupying himself with revisions of his earlier books, and particularly *Lavengro* and *The Romany Rye*.

G. K. Chesterton (1874–1936) is commemorated at **11 Warwick Gardens, W14**, but spent only part of his boyhood there. **W. H. Hudson** (1841–1922) is remembered for spending his last years at **40 St Luke's Road, W11** dying there on August 18 1922, and **Sir Leslie Stephen** is recalled by a plaque on the walls of his old home at **22 Hyde Park Gate, SW7** just a few doors away from the house of **Robert Baden-Powell**, founder of the Boy Scout movement. **Sir Leslie Stephen** is mentioned at greater length in the section on Bloomsbury, (see page 89).

No less a distinguished literary circle is commemorated by the plaque to **Ford Madox Ford** (1873–1939), who lived for some years at **80 Campden Hill Road, W8**. Ford, the editor of *The English Review*, enjoyed the friendship of writers like Henry James, Joseph Conrad, H. G. Wells and Arnold Bennett, all of whom visited him here. **South Lodge**, as this house is known in memory of Sir James South, the famous astrologer, who had his observatory nearby in the grounds of Phillimore House, was one of the first serious literary salons in London to herald the talents of Ezra Pound.

Dickinson (1862–1932) **11 Edwardes Square, W8**, author and humanist. **Henry Austin Dobson** (1840–1921) poet and essayist **10 Redcliffe Street, SW10**. **James Froude** (1818–1894) historian and man of letters, lived at **5 Onslow Gardens, SW7**. Close friend of Carlyle's. **George Godwin** (1813–1888) architect, lived at **24 Alexander Square, SW7**. **W. H. Hudson** (1841–1922) spent last years of his life at **40 St Luke's Road, W11**, died there August 18 1922. **Mohammed Ali Jinnah** (1876–1948) founder of Pakistan, stayed at **35 Russell Road, W14** in 1895. **Louis Kossuth** (1802–1894) Hungarian patriot, stayed at **39 Chepstow Villas, W2**. **Andrew Lang** (1844–1912) man of letters, lived at **1 Marloes Road, W8** from 1876–1912. **Sir John Lavery** (1856–1941) lived at **5 Cromwell Place, SW7**. **Andrew Bonar Law** (1858–1923) Prime Minister, **24 Onslow Gardens, SW7**. **William Edward Hartpole Lecky** (1838–1903) **38 Onslow Gardens, SW7**. Historian. **First Baron Lugard** (1858–1945) colonial administrator, lived at **51 Rutland Gate, SW7**. **Stephane Mallarme** (1842–1898) poet, stayed at **6 Brompton Square, SW7**. **Samuel Palmer** (1805–1881) artist lived briefly, rather sporadically, during a ten-year period at **6 Duoro Place, SW7** between 1850–1861. **Sir Nigel Playfair** (1874–1934) **26 Pelham Crescent, SW7**.

FURTHER NAMES COMMEMORATED IN KENSINGTON

Field Marshal (Edmund Henry Hynman) Viscount Allenby (1861–1936) commemorated at **24 Wetherby Gardens, SW5**. **Sir Edwin Arnold** (1832–1904) poet and journalist, commemorated at **31 Bolton Gardens, SW5**. **Sir Max Beerbohm** (1872–1956) artist and writer, is commemorated at **57 Palace Gardens Terrace, W8**. **Charles Booth** (1840–1916) pioneer in social work **6 Grenville Place, SW7**. Mainly remembered for a 17 volume sociological work, *Life and Labour of The People of London*. **Muzio Clementi** (1752–1832) composer, stayed at **128 Kensington Church Street, W8**. **Goldsworthy Lowes**

HAMMERSMITH

Charles Keene (1823–1891) is commemorated at Cadby Hall, Hammersmith Road, W6. Keene, a humorous artist, lived here for nearly thirty years. It was in 1885 that he left his lodgings in Bloomsbury and came to join his mother and sister in Hammersmith. He was then contributing cartoons for *Punch, Illustrated London News* and other popular journals. His studio was in Baker Street, three miles away. His biographer, Layard, tells us: 'He breakfasted about nine o'clock, his meal consisting generally of porridge, bacon cooked to a cinder, fruit tart and jam. He then walked to his studio regardless of the weather, never in the heaviest rain using an umbrella.... There he would remain until eleven or twelve o'clock at night, when he trudged home.' On one occasion he had just arrived home, having trudged through the deserted streets, when some thought convinced him that he had forgotten to turn out the gas in his studio. Rather than spend hard-earned money on a cab, Keene chose to walk all the way back to Baker Street again, only to find that he had locked up properly as usual. Keene loved music. He had a good bass voice and sang in the chorus of the Handel Festival. 'His tuning fork was always ready to hand, and when he chanced to pick up a fragment of old minstelry, he would often begin to hum it over while he breakfasted.' Cheerful, and popular with his fellow artists, he lived here until a short time before his death. The plaque was erected in 1930.

'Ouida' (**Marie Louise de la Ramée**), the novelist (1839–1908), is commemorated at **11 Ravenscourt Square, W6**. She came to London in 1859. It was then that a neighbour gave her an introduction to William Harrison Ainsworth, and her literary career began. Never a writer of any importance, her stay in London was also brief. The following year, 1860, Ouida (the name is a childish misrepresentation of Louise) left for Florence where she lived almost continuously till her death 48 years later.

Sir Frank Short, the engraver (1857–1945) is commemorated at **56 Brook Green, W6** and **Sir Emery Walker**, who had such a profound influence on nineteenth century typographical design, is commemorated at **7 Hammersmith Terrace, W6**.

WESTMINSTER

The City of Westminster extends from Covent Garden in the east to Pimlico in the west. Covering more than eight square miles of central London, there are more commemorative plaques in this part of London than any other, many of them to the politicians who needed to live close to the Houses of Parliament in Westminster itself.

At its centre is Soho, which derives its name, *The Oxford English Dictionary* tells us, from 'an Anglo-French hunting call, probably of a purely exclamatory nature'. William Kent, in his *Encyclopaedia to London* recalls a mention in Machyn that refers to this: 'A good cry for a mylle, and after the hondys kylled the fox at the end of sent Gylle and theyr was a great cry at the deth.' Even today, the Dog and Fox public house in Frith Street remembers this old hunting association.

Soho grew up in pleasant, haphazard fashion. Only gradually were the green fields that ran northwards to the hills of Hampstead dotted about with brick kilns, artisan dwellings and the multifarious workshops of refugee craftsmen. Today, with its restaurants, street markets, studios, foreign foodstores, night clubs, and the bustle of a thriving international film and television business, Soho remains the most cosmopolitan of all London villages. Like Chelsea in the nineteenth century, Soho in the eighteenth attracted many writers to live there. In Gerrard Street, W1, just south of Shaftesbury Avenue **John Dryden** lived. Although the commemorative plaque identifies Dryden with **43 Gerrard Street, W1**, it is virtually certain that he occupied the house next door, to the east, **No. 44**. Dryden moved here from Long Acre, in nearby Covent Garden,

Karl Marx's small flat in Dean Street, W1, marked in this photograph by the position of his commemorative plaque (erected in 1967), stands above one of London's most celebrated restaurants.

in 1687. 'My House', he wrote to a friend, 'is in Gerrard Street, the fifth door on the left hand side, comeing [sic] from Newport Street.' The commemorative plaque was erected as long ago as 1870 by The Royal Society of Arts, and by the time their mistake had been realised and rectified by the London County Council, who by then had taken over the Blue Plaque scheme, his real residence, at No. 44, had been pulled down. Even so, glimpses of his life there remain for us. Spence, in his book *Anecdotes of Books and Men* (1820) declares that, 'Dryden most commonly used to write in the ground room next to the street'. Perhaps Dryden worked here on purpose. To have moved to the rear of the house would have been too distracting. The gardens of Leicester House, a royal residence, backed onto his own, and presented, according to Dryden, 'the best prospect of the house'. By the time Dryden came to live here, his great satirical poems and plays had all been written. The years that he spent here were devoted to the translation of the classics, Virgil's the *Iliad*, some of Ovid's *Metamorphoses*, as well as Chaucer and Boccaccio.

It was during these labours that his house was damaged by a great gale in the autumn of 1698, which scattered the trees in the gardens of Leicester House and which 'blew down three of my chimneys and dismantled all one side of my house by throwing down the tiles'. Luckily for Dryden, he had just made an agreement with his publisher for £300, so the repair bill may not have caused him too much hardship after all.

Edmund Burke (1729–1797) who is commemorated in **37 Gerrard Street, W1**, was another who used to work at the front of his house. J. T. Smith, a painter and antiquary, and a neighbour of Burke's recalls in his book, *A Book for a Rainy Day*: 'Many a time when I had no inclination to go to bed at the dawn of day, I have looked down from my window to see whether the author of *Sublime and Beautiful* had left his drawing room, where I had seen the great orator many a night after he had left the House of Commons, seated at a table covered with papers, attended by an amanuensis who sat opposite him.' Though Burke was the only politician to be commemorated in Soho, he was by no means the only political thinker. Greatest of the others who are commemorated is, of course, **Karl Marx** (1818–1883) who is remembered at **28 Dean Street, W1.**

Marx lodged here, in two small rooms, it is thought on the top floor, with his family for five-and-a-half years from 1851–1856. He had arrived in England in August 1849 after the collapse of the revolutionary movement of 1848 in the Rhineland. His previous lodgings had been at The German Hotel in Leicester Square, then staying briefly at another house in Dean Street – No. 64. It was here he had produced with Engels the last disputatious numbers of the *Neue Rheinische Zeitung.*

When Marx and his family moved to No. 28, the *Survey of London* tells us, the main occupants of the house were an Italian born cook, an Italian confectioner, and a teacher of languages. In the 1851 census Marx appears as Charles Marks, and is accredited as a 'political author'. Marx had a wretched time in these two rooms. He was terribly poor, and the awful sickness which was so inevitable in such overcrowded conditions caused the death of no less than three of the young children. That he was able to spend so much time studying at the British Museum at this period, as well as contributing to journals like the *Peoples' Paper*, and the *New York Tribune*, says a great deal for his stamina, and steely determination. A report of a Prussian Agent gives a glimpse of the crowded disorder in which Marx and his family survived at 28 Dean Street. The flat, the report ran, was: 'in one of the worst, and therefore also the cheapest quarters of London. He occupies two rooms; and in the whole apartment there is not one clean and good piece of furniture to be found. All is broken,

tattered and torn, everywhere clings thick dust, everywhere is the greatest disorder ... his manuscripts, books and newspapers lie beside the children's toys, bits and pieces from his wife's workbasket, tea cups with broken rims, dirty spoons, knives, forks, lamps, an inkwell, tumblers, dutch clay pipes, tobacco ash ... all this on the same table ...; sitting down is really a hazardous business ... but all this gives Marx and his wife not the slightest embarrassment; one is received in the friendliest way.'

As soon as the Marx family could afford to move from this 'old hovel', they did so, and in September 1856 Marx wrote to Engels that they were in 'einen wahren hurly burly' with the removal, and by October of that year they were installed at No. 9, later 46 Grafton Terrace, St Pancras, where at least things were rather more comfortable for them all.

Some fifty years later but only a few doors and one street away from Marx's dwelling in Dean Street, television was first demonstrated to the cream of The British Institution. The occasion was Friday, January 27 1926, and the place, also commemorated by a plaque, was a small, back room attic at **22 Frith Street, W1.** Television's demonstrator on this occasion was **John Logie Baird**, a young man who for some years, in Hastings in Sussex, had been experimenting with transmitting and receiving recognisable images with their graduations of light and shade. He was 34, and a shareholder in a new company called Television Ltd, which had been formed with a capital of a mere £500. At Hastings, his equipment had been constructed with such primitive objects as old tea chests which formed a base to carry the motor which rotated a circular cardboard disc. Other pieces of this first television machinery – for that is what it was – were discs cut out of the cardboard from an old hat box; darning needles serving as spindles; biscuit tins to house the projection lamps. On being forced to leave his premises in Hastings he arrived in London, determined to show off his invention to the broadcasting world. Thus it was, as Gordon Ross has written: '... that more than 40 members of the British Institution, many of them distinguished scientists, and all of them in full evening dress, arrived in Frith Street. They climbed three flights of stone stairs and then stood in a narrow draughty passage while batches of six at a time were brought into the two tiny attic rooms which formed the laboratory.'

Though **Wolfgang Mozart** (1756–1791) is commemorated elsewhere in Westminster by the plaque at **121 Ebury Street, SW1**, it is from his time as a boy, whilst living at 20 Frith Street, that one of the most charming recollections about him comes. Wolfgang Mozart was aged eight when he, his father and sister were staying with Thomas Williamson, as lodgers. In March 1765, the following advertisement appeared in *The Public Advertiser:* 'Mr Mozart, the father of the celebrated musical family who have so justly raised the admiration of the greatest musicians of Europe, proposes to give the public an opportunity of hearing these young prodigies perform both in public and private, by giving on the thirteenth of this month, a concert which will chiefly be conducted by his son, a boy of eight years of age, with all the overtures of his own composition. Tickets may be had at 5 shillings each at Mr Mozart's in Thrift Street, Soho, where Ladies and Gentlemen will find the family at home everyday of the week from 12 o'clock to 2 o'clock and have an opportunity of putting his talents to a more particular proof by giving him anything to play at sight in any music without a bass, which he will write upon the spot without recurring to his harpsicord.' Far from boasting, Mr Mozart, if anything was under-selling the genius of his young prodigy. Though Wolfgang stayed here in Thrift Street for only a year, he still had time to compose several symphonies, including his K.19, 19d, 20, 21, as well as several more. From this address his Opus 3 (K. 10–15) was dedicated to Queen Charlotte.

Advertising seems also to have been an attractive means of selling for **Antonio Canaletto**, who lodged at **41 Beak Street, W1**, for two years from 1749–1751, where he is also commemorated. A newspaper advertisement of July 26 1749 states: 'Signor Canaletto hereby invites any gentleman that will be pleased to come to his house to see a picture done by him, being a "View of St James's Park", which he hopes in some measure may deserve their appropriation.' A similar advertisement of two years later, just before his return to Italy, refers to a 'representation of Chelsea College, Ranelagh House and The River Thames'.

Success may have attended Mozart and Canaletto during their time in Soho but not so **William Hazlitt** (1778–1830) the essayist, who is commemorated at **6 Frith Street, W1**. Hazlitt spent only six months in Soho, alas the last of his life. He died soured and embittered, separated from his wife, harrassed financially through the failure of his publishers, and altogether broken and dispirited. He had moved here from lodgings in Bouverie Street. A critic of genius, and a brilliant essayist, he was as Thomas Talfourd, a contemporary, vividly put it, 'worn by sickness and thought'. Shortly after coming to Frith Street he was attacked by a violent sort of cholera, and he never rallied from it. 'He died so quietly' said his grandson, 'that his son, who was sitting by his bedside, did not know that he was gone until the vital breath had been extinct a moment or two.' He was buried in St Anne's churchyard, with Charles Lamb and P. G. Patmore the only mourners.

John Hunter (1728–1793) who is commemorated at **31 Golden Square, W1,** and was seen as a man who, as G. T. Bettany wrote of him in the *Dictionary of National Biography*, 'as an in-

Right: Richard Sheridan's plaque at the entrance of his home, above another now well-known name more closely associated with the present fame of Savile Row.

vestigator, original thinker, and stimulator of thought, stands at the head of British Surgeons'. Hunter lived at a house on this site, where he also practised as a surgeon and formed a private class for anatomy and operative surgery. Born in East Kilbride, Lanarkshire in 1728, he studied medicine at the Chelsea Hospital, then St Bartholomew's, finally becoming a surgeon's pupil at St George's Hospital, where he worked under his older brother, William Hunter. The process of surgery fascinated Hunter. While other men of his time were bent on exploring foreign seas and distant continents, Hunter sensed that some of the greatest discoveries of that time lay within the human frame. The topography of the human body, and the causes of its various internal disorders, became his greatest interest. A lifetime of research and study was his great contribution to the increasingly scientific understanding of curative medicine. Of course, this interest was not fostered without an adequate supply of bodies on which to make his investigations! A dying tiger which Hunter once bought for dissection purposes, having borrowed the necessary five guineas purchase fee from the King's bookseller, could not have appreciated how much his eventual fate contributed to surgical knowledge as Hunter's skilled hands carefully probed the contours, shapes and directions of its organic systems.

Alas, such knowledge did not calm one O'Brien, or O'Byrne, who, in 1783 became the most expensive specimen Hunter had ever acquired. O'Brien was an Irish giant, seven feet and seven inches in height. His huge shape fascinated the squat and rugged Hunter. He was determined to own the dying Irishman for his experiments. But the giant, not unnaturally, was petrified by the proposed fate of his huge body. One can imagine the poor man's agonised face as the first overtures were made for his acquisition. Hunter must have appeared as some sort of fiendish monster as he gloated over the Irishman's gigantic form, dreaming of the discoveries he would make inside. Determined to outwit Hunter, the Irishman declared in his will that upon death, his body was to be sealed in a coffin and sunk immediately in deep water. But Hunter was already one step ahead of such an eventuality. He had already bribed the undertaker. For the huge sum of £500, the undertaker allowed Hunter to steal the body while it was on its way down to the sea. It was promptly taken by Hunter to his house in his carriage, and rapidly skeletonised.

'Hunter', Bettany tells us, 'was of middle height, vigorous and robust, with high shoulders and squat neck. His hair in youth was a reddish yellow, and in later years white.' He was an exhaustive worker, often rising at five o'clock in the morning to dissect for four hours before breakfast. In the evening, after a day spent seeing his patients, he would be back at his bench once more, often working as late as midnight. **William Hunter** (1718–1783) the anatomist and elder brother of John Hunter, has the site of his home commemorated by a plaque on the walls of the **Lyric Theatre**, in **Great Windmill Street, W1**. Part of the old house, which also served as a museum, was incorporated into the building of the theatre itself, its three storeys of rooms serving as dressing rooms at the rear of the auditorium. William, though a Fellow of the Royal Society, and Physician Extraordinary to Queen Charlotte, and indeed eminent in every way, is by no means as memorable a person as his younger brother, with whom he did not enjoy a close relationship. The two men quarrelled, squabbling over the credit for discoveries made in the human body. William was an avid collector. Apart from the various specimens in his museum, which also served as part of his school of anatomy, there were also coins and medals, minerals, shells, corals, and a remarkable collection of rare and valuable Greek and Latin books. In acquiring this collection, he also gained the reputation of

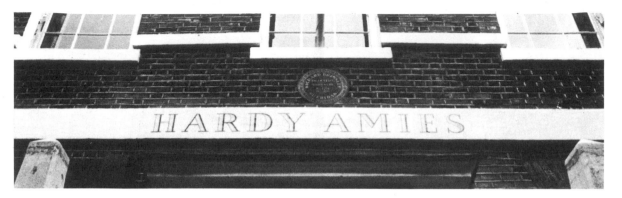

being a hard, even greedy man to deal with. But, like his brother, he was utterly single-minded in his profession.

Yet one more great figure from the English scientific renaissance lived in Soho, **Sir Joseph Banks** (1743–1820) commemorated at **32 Soho Square, W1**. Banks, who became President of the Royal Society, was also responsible for the foundation of the Linnean Society, which met here for many years. Banks, who was born in Westminster in 1743, was a man who believed in travelling to gather the botanical specimens that so fascinated him. In 1768 he accompanied Captain Cook on an expedition to Newfoundland. His house back in London was kept by his sister, and it was here, some years later, that he happened to mention to a young medical student called Smith, later Sir John Smith, that he had been offered the manuscript and botanical collections of Linnaeus, the great Swedish botanist, but that he had declined to purchase them. Smith, full of zeal and interest immediately badgered his father to advance him the necessary sum of £1,000, and in 1784 the treasure arrived in London, packed in up to 26 cases. Edward Walford, in his book, *Old and New London*, recounts that King Gustavus of Sweden, who had been absent in France, was much displeased to hear on his return that a vessel had just sailed for England bearing the collection of the far-famed naturalist. Smith was later made a Fellow of the Royal Society for his foresight in making the acquisition. The collection, then housed at 32 Soho Square, made Banks's residence even more important as a meeting place for many of the key scientists of the day. His habit was to hold breakfast parties, after which the guests would drift into his great library at the rear of the house, next to the room that contained his large and adventurous natural history collection. When Sir Charles Bell, another resident of Soho Square, W1, breakfasted there in 1804, he found that his host had 'a set of most absurd animals about him – living animals – German and French toadeaters'!

Like William Hunter, Banks was another habitual collector. Horace Walpole once related that Banks fascinated one breakfast party by a small snuffbox out of which a colourful singing bird used to spring when it was opened, and immediately wanted one for himself. It is reasonable to assume that he would frequently glance his collector's eye into the windows of the pawnshop then standing at 143 Wardour Street, just around the corner, in the hope of picking up a pleasing bargain. Had he ever ventured into the pawnshop, and fingered some of the goods there, it is more likely than not that he would have come across some of the few remaining objects of worth owned by Sheridan, the dramatist, who, towards the end of his life was so heavily in debt that he paid frequent visits there.

Richard Brinsley Butler Sheridan (1751–1816) is commemorated at **14 Savile Row, W1**. Dramatist, wit, most brilliant of parliamentary orators, and sometime principal proprietor of the Drury Lane Theatre, Sheridan lived all the time beyond his means, borrowing, getting into debt, and cheerfully dodging the bailiffs who were soon only too familiar with his name. Charming, and funny, he was always in demand as a companion. After one particularly heavy night out, Byron wrote of him in his diary: 'What a wreck that man is! And all from bad pilotage: for no one had ever better gales, though now and again a little too squally. Poor dear Sherry! I shall never know how Kinnaird and I conducted Sheridan down a damned corkscrew staircase, which had certainly been constructed before the discovery of fermented liquors, and to which no legs, however crooked, could possibly accommodate themselves. We deposited him safe at home where his man, evidently used to the business, waited to receive him in the hall.'

Just a year later, he was dying £5,000 in debt,

Below: *A rare photograph of one of the original Royal Society of Arts plaques. This one, erected in 1875, decorates the house occupied by Sir Joshua Reynolds. The house, on the west side of Leicester Square, has now been demolished.*
Right: *The striking entrance to Gainsborough's house in Pall Mall.*
Below right: *An unusual view of Gainsborough's Pall Mall mansion, showing the enormous size of the painter's home.*

and only saved from the bailiffs by the emphatic intervention of the doctor who was attending him on his deathbed. The bailiffs wanted to carry him off to a 'sponging house' in his blankets there and then. As it was, they had to content themselves with the following epitaph against his name in an official file, 'Goods distrained by Sheriff. Distraint resisted. Dead and insolvent'!

George Grote (1794–1871) also commemorated by a plaque in Savile Row, this time at **12 Savile Row, W1**, was very far from suffering such intrusions. The great Greek historian, Fellow of the Royal Society, and Vice-Chancellor of London University, lived a much more respectable and contented life. Lovingly looked after by his wife, who was a charming hostess, Grote moved here in 1848. A man of regular habits, and unpretentious discipline, he used to write throughout the day in the front parlours which had been turned into offices. The Rev. P. Anton, in his book *The Masters of History*, tells us how Grote's favourite dog, Dora, took up a position on his knee as he worked. 'The greater portion of Grote's volumes on Plato were written over the back of his little favourite.' The evenings were just as restful too. Receptions were held here frequently, Jenny Lind and Chopin being amongst those who gave recitals to the guests.

Moving back to Soho again, we note the plaques to **Arthur Onslow** (1691–1768) Speaker of The House of Commons from 1728–1761, on the site of Fauconberg House at **20 Soho Square, W1**; to the furniture designer **Thomas Sheraton** 1751–1806 who is commemorated at **163 Wardour Street, W1** where he lived for two years from 1793–1795; to **Willy Clarkson**, the famous theatrical wigmaker who lived at **41 Wardour Street, W1**, and to **General John Burgoyne** (1722–1792), who lived and died at **10 Hertford Street, W1**.

Just south of Soho, in Leicester Square, WC2, is a bust to **Sir Joshua Reynolds** (1723–1792) co-founder and First President of the Royal

Society, the site of whose home in the Square is commemorated on the walls of **Fanum House**. He had first lived nearby in St Martin's Lane, but, finding his prospects 'so bright and extensive' had moved to a large house on the north side of Great Newport Street. It was here that he met Dr Johnson for the first time. Reynolds, though slightly deaf, and naturally careless, even Bohemian by contemporary standards, quickly established himself as a favourite painter of all who mattered in fashionable London. Once again he needed more room. In the summer of 1760, then aged 36, he took possession of Leicester Square House, standing in Leicester Fields. In his pocket book he recorded the price he paid, £1,000. The house had a frontage of 28 feet, and extended over 100 feet westward towards Whitcomb Street, where there was a coach-house and stables. His studio was a large room, some 20 feet long by 16 feet broad. His sitter's chair moved sensibly on castors. Reynolds used to enter the studio at ten o'clock, examining designs and touching up unfinished portraits until the first sitter of the day arrived at eleven o'clock. He would paint until mid-afternoon, when he would prepare for the evenings, which were given over to entertaining. Courtney notes, 'a table prepared for seven or eight was often compelled to contain fifteen or sixteen'. It was after one of these evenings, sitting at his fireside, that Reynolds suggested to Johnson the establishment of a club where they could meet sometimes with their friends. This began at the Turks Head in Gerrard Street, where Burke, Goldsmith, Garrick, Fanny Burney, and Boswell were amongst those who gathered regularly for supper and conversation.

Thomas Gainsborough (1727–1788) commemorated by a plaque at **82 Pall Mall, SW1**, moved only on the fringes of Reynolds' circle. He lacked the gaiety Reynolds enjoyed so much in others, and was a much more solitary man. Music was another of Gainsborough's

Below: *An unusual angle of Handel's House in Brook Street, W1.*
Right: *This portrait of George Frederick Handel was painted in 1749 when the composer was 64, and within 10 years of his death.*

pleasures. J. T. Smith wrote in *Nollekens and His Times* of an occasion when Gainsborough seemed to be swept away by the sound of music: 'Upon our arrival at Mr Gainsborough's, the artist was listening to a violin, and held up his fingers as a request for silence. Colonel Hamilton was playing to him in so exquisite a manner that Gainsborough exclaimed "Now, my dear Colonel, if you will but go on, I will give you that picture of the 'Boy At The Stile', which you have so often wished to purchase of me"; a gift which the Colonel – a gentleman who combined an incongruous pre-eminence as an amateur musician and a pugilist – duly carried off on his departure.'

Another prize of Gainsborough's which was swept off, this time without his permission, was his daughter, who left to marry a young music professor who had been a visitor to their home. Reynolds, present at Gainsborough's deathbed, was amused by the painter's last utterance, when the dying Gainsborough muttered to him: 'We are all going to heaven, and Vandyke is one of the company!' Reynolds, for the time being at least, continued to enjoy his earthly pleasures, and in the taverns of Soho in particular.

George Frederick Handel, the German composer who became a naturalised Englishman, is commemorated at **22 Brook Street, W1.** Handel never married, but with Hogarth, was one of the chief benefactors of the Foundling Hospital, in Bloomsbury. Handel presented an organ to this institution, which cared for the homeless. Frequently he conducted the services there, and often visited it to play one of his oratorios, especially *Messiah*, the score of which he left by will to the Hospital for ever. Lysons writes in *Environs of London* that when Handel presided there at his own oratorios, the Hospital was crowded, and as he had persuaded the performers to give their services free, the profits to the Hospital were considerable. Handel, a warm, and friendly man, with dark

This reproduction of an old portrait of Benjamin Franklin was painted in 1790 when he was 84 years old. The painting is in possession of the Pennsylvania Historical Society.

and heavy eyebrows, never mastered the English language properly. He also had an enormous appetite. Wilmot Harrison, writing in 1889, quotes an amusing occasion when Handel was dining alone one day in a tavern. He had ordered a dinner which, in the ordinary way, would have been enough to satisfy three persons. When the meal did not arrive, he inquired impatiently the reasons for the delay. 'I am waiting for your company to arrive, sir' said the serving girl. 'Ach!' Handel replied somewhat testily. 'Pring up te tinner prestissimo. I am de company!'

The German poet and essayist **Heinrich Heine** (1799–1856) is commemorated at **32 Craven Street, WC2,** where he stayed in 1827. Heine did not enjoy his visit to London a great deal. He wrote complainingly to his friend Friedrich Merckel, 'it is snowing outside, and there is no fire in my chimney . . . I am very peevish and ill to boot . . . I have seen and heard much, but have not had a clear view of anything . . . living here is terribly dead. So far I have spent more than a guinea a day . . . it is so frightfully damp and uncomfortable here, and no one understands me, and no one understands German!'

Another visitor to London, who also lodged in Craven Street, this time at **36 Craven Street, WC2,** where he too is commemorated, was **Benjamin Franklin** (1706–1790) the great American statesman, diplomat and scientist. He seemed similarly affected by London of that time. Writing to a friend he declared: 'The whole town is one great smoaky [sic] house and every street a chimney, the air full of floating sea coal soot, and you never get a sweet breath of what is pure without riding some miles into the country.' Franklin had settled here soon after his arrival in 1757 as agent to The General Assembly of Pennsylvania. He brought with him his son, taking up lodgings with a Mrs Stevenson, who had been recommended to him by some friends at home in America. Franklin and she soon became firm friends, and Fisher

writes in *The True Benjamin Franklin* 'for her daughter he formed a strong attachment which continued all his life'. Franklin had yet more soot to worry about when a fire in the street destroyed two of the houses. 'Our house and yard were covered in falling coals of fire, but as it rain'd hard nothing catch'd.' In 1762 Franklin returned to America, hoping for an early retirement, but such an able negotiator and diplomat could not be spared in the troubled years leading up to the American Declaration of Independence. In 1764 he was back again petitioning Parliament once more about the key issues of the day. Franklin tried to take a middle course in his duties, with the result that he was accused in America of being too much an Englishman, and in England of being too much an American. But life was not all hard-bitten diplomacy. By now he enjoyed a wide circle of English friends, including David Garrick and Adam Smith the Scottish economist. Also his fame as a scientist had brought him various commissions in London, the most spectacular of which was the erecting of lightning rods on St Paul's Cathedral, and also on the Government Powder stocks. Franklin left London in 1772.

Over a hundred years later, in 1890, another famous person commemorated by a plaque was complaining about the fog in this immediate area. He was **Rudyard Kipling** (1865–1936) remembered at **43 Villiers Street, WC2.** He had arrived in London in September 1890 with 'fewer pounds in his pocket than he cared to remember'. London, after India where he had worked as a journalist, and then America, he found very cold, and the thick pea-souper fogs foul and horrible. 'Once', he wrote in his autobiography, 'I faced the reflection of my own face in the jet black mirror of the window panes for five days'. He took three rooms here in Villiers Street. 'My rooms were small, not overclean or well kept, but from my desk I could look out of my window through the

fanlights of Gatti's music hall entrance, across the street, almost onto its stage. The Charing Cross trains rumbled through my dreams on one side, the boom of the Strand on the other, while, before my windows, Father Thames under The Shot Tower walked up and down with his traffic.' Poor Kipling may have been at this time, but he never had need to go hungry. His rooms 'were above an establishment of Harris, the Sausage King, who, for tuppence, gave us as much sausage and mash as would carry us from breakfast to dinner'. Occasionally, in the evening, feeling he could spare a few pennies more, he would visit Gatti's Music Hall, accompanied by 'an elderly, but upright barmaid from a pub nearby'. It was this same barmaid who, on one occasion, bombarded Kipling with the story of a friend ''oo was mistook in 'er man' thereby providing him with the inspiration for the poem *Mary Pity Women*. Of Gatti's, Kipling recalls, 'the smoke, the roar and good fellowship of relaxed humanity set the scheme for a certain sort of song'. The infectious rhythms of the English music hall songs, and their earthy humour, coming freshly on the ears of a young man in his mid-twenties, formed the genesis of the *Barrack Room Ballads*, which soon started to take shape in his mind. The following year, in 1891, Kipling's health broke down. 'All my Indian microbes joined hands and sang for a month in the darkness of Villiers Street.' He then travelled again, to Italy, New Zealand, Australia and South Africa, married, and settled in America for a time in New England where the Jungle Books were written. On Kipling's eventual return to England in 1899, he took a house in Rottingdean, in Sussex, finally moving to the Bateman's, at Burwash in the same county, where the house has been preserved as a remarkable museum to one of the best loved of English writers. He died in January 1936, and was buried in Westminster Abbey. This plaque in Villiers Street was erected in May 1940.

Top: *This portrait by Burne-Jones shows Kipling at work in his study in Rottingdean.*
Bottom: *Kipling's House in Villiers Street, a large gaunt building that faces the Arts Theatre, formerly Gatti's Music Hall. When Kipling lived here as a young man, the narrow view across the road to the entrance to Gatti's was frequently obscured by thick London fog, helped by the thick coal smoke from the trains at Charing Cross Station, and the passage of shipping on the Thames only a few yards from his front door. The memories of his visits to Gatti's Music Hall were to inspire him to write some of his most popular poetry.*

Unlike Kipling, **George Moore** (1852–1933) the author who is commemorated at **121 Ebury Street, SW1**, travelled little during his lifetime. Born in County Mayo, in 1852, he had plans to become a painter, and twenty years later, after his father's death, went to Paris to study painting, but in the ten years he was there his aspirations turned towards literature. His occupation of this house began in 1911, and he was to spend the rest of his life there.

'I am in London and am renting this house', he wrote in a letter to Edward DuJardin, 'or rather this little hole in which to carry on my authorship.' Moore's apathy towards his home seemed to continue, and even after eight years of being there, he was still writing feebly, 'the most I can hope for to relieve the monotony of Ebury Street, a long narrow slum, in which I took a house in the Coronation Year, is a new idea'. Despite these disgruntled sentiments, he continued to stay there, and, over the years, the house acquired a flavour and character all of its own. Even the faithful maid, Clara, stayed, opening the door to Moore's visitors, who included Walter de la Mare and Edmund Gosse. C. Lewis Hind wrote about his own visits there: 'Whenever I think of George Moore, I see him in an armchair by his fireside stroking his cat, and allowing his extraordinary mind to reflect on the past.' Moore himself, who wrote extensively during these years, commented on his innermost reflections, 'My body is in 121 Ebury Street, my soul in the Val Changis'. Perhaps he also liked Paris for another reason, the absence of the large number of dogs who were allowed to foul the streets outside his London home. Moore found in this insanitary malpractice an excuse to vent his tetchiness often and loudly to the authorities. Geraint Goodwin, in *Conversations with George Moore* recalls: '. . . although he was obliged to use a typewriter in his later work, he would not tolerate a telephone. A fire was almost a necessity to him, even in the mildest

weather, and visitors usually found him sitting or lying by one.' One of the last recorded recollections of George Moore, made by his friend Charles Morgan shortly before Moore's death in 1933, still paints a melancholy picture of the Irish writer. 'It was a winter's morning. A large blind was across the window; the dining table had been moved; George Moore lay in the middle of the room under a blaze of an electric chandelier. . . . He began to tell of the book he was then writing and hoped to finish, *A Communication To My Friends*, finding it an occasion to speak of his early life and his struggle with the circulating libraries . . . when it was time to leave him we stood at the door, he cried out "Come again? Come separately or come together, but come. All day I lie here alone. All day alone".'

Benjamin Disraeli (1804–1881) statesman and author, is commemorated at **19 Curzon Street, W1**, where he lived for only the last few months of his life. His association with the house seems bleak. For most of his life he had lived in Park Lane, at the house owned by his wife. On her death in 1872, he had moved to Whitehall Gardens, and then, on his retirement from active politics, to Curzon Street. Before his parliamentary career Disraeli had been a busy novelist. *Vivian Grey; Contarini Fleming; Wondrous Tale of Alroy* and *Henrietta Temple* had all been published before he took his seat at Westminster. *Coningsby* and *Sybil* were published in the 1840s, and it was not until he began sensing retirement that he commenced writing his last novel, *Endymion*. It was with the £10,000 gained from the rights of this novel, published in 1880, that he secured the nine-year lease of this house. From Francis Espinasse's *Literary Recollections*, we are told the house had, 'a look of spick and span newness, with no pictures, and no busts or engravings, only a few pieces of Dresden China'.

William Gladstone (1809–1898) commemorated at **11 Carlton House Terrace, W1**, lived here for almost

Top: *Millais's portrait of Disraeli.*
Bottom: *Gladstone from the London sketchbook.*
Right: *A recruiting poster from the First World War, showing Lord Kitchener in dictatorial pose.*
Far right: *A portrait of Samuel Pepys by John Hayls, 1666.*

20 years, selling when he resigned from office as Prime Minister in 1875, in his sixty-sixth year. 'I had grown to the house', he wrote, 'having lived in it more than any other since I was born.' In a letter to his wife in February of that year he added the reason for his sadness at leaving: 'So much has occurred there, and thus it is leaving not the house only, but the neighbourhood, where I have been with you for more then 35 years, and altogether nearly 40.' By the neighbourhood, he meant other houses where he and his wife had lived before settling at Carlton House Terrace, including, of course, 10 Downing Street. Occasionally the Cabinet met at Carlton House Terrace instead of Downing Street. In March 1873, he wrote to the Queen, 'Cabinet met informally at this house at 2 p.m. and sat till 5½'. Here too he wrote and published his *Studies in Homer and the Homeric Age* while continuing his studies on religous and other subjects. It was from this house that he ventured forth into the streets in nearby Piccadilly, moved to offer help to young prostitutes. In fact there is some doubt whether Gladstone, on these sorties into London's twilight world, was acting solely from wholesome Christian motives. Whatever the reason, it was fortunate for Gladstone that politics, both domestically and internationally, was still something of a courtly exercise in his day.

Lord Kitchener (1850–1916) is remembered at **2 Carlton Gardens, SW1.** He was appointed Secretary of State for War in 1914, and that Christmas was the first one he had spent in his native country for 40 years. Before that he had been living in every outpost of the Empire. The house at 2 Carlton Gardens is commemorated not because it was his residence, but because it was from here that he masterminded his massive recruitment campaign at the beginning of the First World War. 'He sat' wrote Lord Eldon, 'his large tortoiseshell spectacles gleaming over his work, baffling weary officials who stood his presence.' Kitchener needed to drive

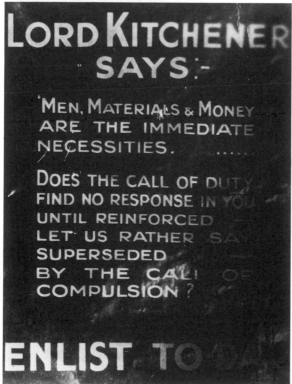

his officials in his vital work of raising new armies. 'His habits were regular and simple. Punctually at 9 a.m. his massive figure, in the blue undress uniform of Field-Marshal, which at that time he wore, was seen ascending the stairway. He ate little, and, following the King's example, had banished alcohol from his table.' He returned home to York House, St James's Palace, which had been lent to him by the King, rarely before 8 p.m. This arduous work, resulting in the famous 'Your Country Needs You' campaign, was to last until his sudden death through drowning when H.M.S. *Hampshire* sank off the Orkneys.

Samuel Pepys (1633–1703) who has plaques to his memory at Nos. **12 and 14 Buckingham Street, WC2,** was Secretary to the Admiralty during his tenure here. He had taken the lease of No. 12 in 1677, but only two years later he had been denounced as a papist and sent to the Tower. On his release from there, he returned to the house in Buckingham Street which his faithful clerk, Hewer, had maintained in his absence.

Lord Nelson (1758–1805), is commemorated at **103 New Bond Street, W1,** where he lived for a time in 1798. Previously, he had lodged for a while in a house standing on a site of the building standing at No. 147. Nelson was a convalescent during his time here, suffering intense pain from the loss of his right arm in a recent naval engagement at Santa Cruz. He was being nursed by Lady Nelson. Southey writes: 'One night he retired early to bed in the hope of enjoying some respite by laudanum [which is a mixture of opium dissolved in alcohol]. He was at that time lodging in Bond Street, and the family were soon disturbed by a mob knocking loudly and violently at the door. The news of Duncan's victory had been made public, and the house was not illuminated; but when the mob were told that Admiral Nelson lay there in bed badly wounded, the foremost of them made answer ''You shall hear no more from us tonight''.'

Left: *Nelson in his cabin on H.M.S. 'Victory' on the eve of Trafalgar.*

Lord Clive of India (1725–1774) commemorated at **45 Berkeley Square, W1,** who had died a quarter of a century before, was another who had used laudanum. In his case, however, the opium doses were self administered, and large ones. Clive, who boasted that, 'between the ages of 24 and 44 he had saved a province, conquered a kingdom, and substituted in the management of its affairs order for anarchy and justice for violence', put an end to his life on November 22 1774. According to an early biographer, Malcom, he had long suffered a painful internal disorder, and for some days before the end paroxysms of agony had caused him to swallow still larger quantities. 'It may well, therefore, be supposed', wrote E. Beresford Chancellor, in *The History of the Squares of London,* 'that the remedy, while alleviating the pain, produced a mental stupour which caused the loss of all self control'; while Macaulay reminds us that, 'his strong mind was fast sinking under many kinds of suffering'. In his essay on Clive Macaulay writes: 'It is with very different feelings we contemplate the spectacle of a great mind ruined by the weariness of satiety, by the pangs of wounded honour, by fatal diseases, and more fatal remedies.' The addiction to opium, the political mischief stirred up against him by some of his adversaries, all became too much for Clive to bear any longer. Horace Walpole styled him: 'that second Kouli Khan' for being the founder of the British Indian Empire. Dr Johnson was even more damning, for Clive, in his opinion, was a man who 'had yet acquired his fortune by such crimes that his consciousness of this impelled him to cut his own throat, because he was weary of still life, little things not being sufficient to move his great mind'. Clive was just in his forty-ninth year.

At **46 Clarges Street, W1, Charles James Fox** is commemorated by a plaque. Elected to Parliament first at the age of 19, as member for Midhurst, he was a brilliant orator. Burke called him 'the greatest debater the world ever saw'. He was also renowned as a man about town, eating and gambling being his particular weaknesses. The Prince Regent got himself elected to Brook's Club, one of Fox's favourite haunts, solely for the sake of making a better acquaintance with him.

Napoleon III, Emperor of France, is commemorated at **1c King Street, St James's, SW1,** where he lived from 1846 until 1848. Here he whiled away difficult days collecting family portraits, books and portfolios, anxiously awaiting news of Louis Philippe's defeat in France. These were difficult days for the European aristocracy. Even the British establishment was threatened by the fervour of revolution. 'Nothing can be more amiable or more well bred than the Emperor's manner', wrote Queen Victoria of him in her diary. Perhaps it was out of gratitude to the cordial welcome he had received from her and others of her family that Napoleon enlisted as a Special Constable to defy the mobs then threatening good order in the London streets.

The plaque to **Henry Fielding** (1707–1754), the novelist stands on the site of the old **Magistrates House** in **Bow Street, WC2.** Fielding, the man who had created the English novel, who had shaken the theatre with laughter, and then had proved immensely effective as a political pamphleteer, had been rewarded for his services with the appointment of Magistrate at Bow Street, then one of the most crowded, congested and most criminally infested quarters of London. Fielding, then aged 43, might have expected better as a reward for his pre-eminence as a man of letters. But undeterred, he threw himself into the duties that were to carry him through the last five years of his life.

The geography of the Strand, Covent Garden, and Bow Street at that time was of the greatest assistance to the footpad, the murderer and the thief. With its narrow alleyways, courtyards, lanes and crowded thoroughfares there were whole districts, in Fielding's words which, 'had they been intended for the very purpose of concealment, they could hardly have been better contrived. Upon such a view, the whole appears as a vast wood or forest, in which a thief may harbour with as great security as wild beasts do in the deserts of Africa or Arabia'. London was in the grips, not so much of a crime epidemic, but of a criminal way of life. Prosecutors were bribed or terrorised, and 'rotten members of the law' were ready to bring before the court false alibis in numbers so great that few prosecutions ever succeeded. In addition, the criminals themselves were well organised 'incorporated in one body, with officers and a treasury'. Fielding's ancient house in Bow Street, with its living quarters upstairs, and the courthouse beneath, became the centre of a ceaseless campaign against all this crime and violence. He frequently sat up all night with the officers from a military unit discussing tactics against the next day's rioters. Fielding needed the help of the military on these occasions. There was no police force. The only representatives of the law to be found in the streets were the officers of the Watch. Fielding himself has told us how these were old men, barely capable of carrying the 'pole' they were armed with, often recruited because of their sheer infirmities, and their inability to practise any other employment. In their feeble hands was entrusted the guardianship of peace when those breaking it had the pistol, the bludgeon and the cutlass amongst their most usual weapons. The author of *Tom Jones*, part of which had been written in Bow Street, now turned his pen to such pamphlets as, '*An enquiry into the causes of the late increase of robbers with some proposals for remedying this growing evil*'. So skilfully and passionately did Fielding argue for reform, and so graphically did he describe the savagery in London's Streets that within six months of the pamphlet's publication new laws 'for better

preventing thefts and robberies', and 'for better preventing the horrid crime of murder' were already being drawn up. Fielding himself, by this time, was already dead. Sir John Fielding, his blind brother, also a magistrate, continued this reforming zeal.

Others commemorated through their associations with Bow Street are **Grinling Gibbons**, the woodcarver, **Charles Macklin**, the physician; and **William Wycherley**, the dramatist.

Nearby, in 1775, J. M. W. Turner, the painter, was born at 26 Maiden Lane, WC2, where his father kept a small barber's shop. The house is long rebuilt now, but it was when accompanying his father one day to a Mr Tomkinson's, where the barber was engaged to friz a wig that Turner, then only a small boy, sat gazing at a silver salver in the room. On the salver, emblazoned with the Tomkinson Arms, was engraved a rampant lion. 'All that day', Walter Thornbury wrote accounting for the time Turner had returned home, 'he sits upstairs all apart, brooding over a sheet of paper. Mother wonders what ails him; Father is consulted at tea-time; and they call for Billy, who with impetuosity produces his paper and exhibits a not unintelligible lion, twin brother to the royal and wilder one on the salver at Mr Tomkinson's. The Gods be praised – the boy is a genius!' From then on, the boy's fate was fixed. Whenever his father was asked in the shop about his son, the answer always was 'It's all settled, sir. William is going to be a painter'. And so it proved. Though his parents had little money, they arranged for him to be apprenticed first to an architectural school, after to an art academy in St Martin's Lane. Some of Turner's father's friends were actors, then playing in Sheridan's comedies at Drury Lane. Through them, Sir Joshua Reynolds met and encouraged him. Years later, a wealthy man, Turner was not to forget his old father. He took him to live with him in Marylebone. There the old man happily spent his last years stretching

J. M. W. Turner, 1775–1851, drawn by Charles Martin.

canvases and mixing paints for the son whose genius he had once nourished.

Another artist, **Thomas Rowlandson**, the caricaturist, is commemorated at **16 John Adam Street, WC2,** where his house existed on this site. **The Adelphi**, as this area is known, is the latinised form of the Greek word for brothers, and a plaque exists here commemorating **Robert and James Adam**, the Scottish architects who built Adelphi Terrace in 1768–1774. The present building stands on this site, the original Terrace buildings having been demolished in 1936. Famous residents in the Terrace included Topham, friend of Dr Johnson; David Garrick, actor; Richard d'Oyly Carte, the Savoy opera promoter; Thomas Hardy, the poet and novelist, also an architect, who studied here under Sir Arthur Blomfield, and George Bernard Shaw, author and playwright. The original London School of Economics, and The Savage Club, also had their premises here.

Isaac Newton, greatest of all natural philosophers, is commemorated at **87 Jermyn Street, SW1**. The premises were rebuilt, and the plaque refixed in 1915. The area in Newton's time was still almost rural, and the hounds still hunted across the fields towards the north of his residence. During his time here, Newton was engaged in an official capacity, carrying out a re-coinage of the gold, silver and copper of the realm. During his 13 years in this house, he also retained his Chair of Mathematics at Cambridge, as well as working on a new edition of *Principia*. He needed the six servants he employed to meet the demands of such a busy life. Here he frequently entertained as well, though taking only a frugal diet for himself. In 1697, he moved to Chelsea.

At **Essex House**, commemorated by a plaque in Essex Street, off the Strand, lived a large number of prominent men of this time. Pepys called it 'a large but ugly house', and certainly by the time he knew it the place had undergone many additions and alterations from the time

A literary party at Sir Joshua Reynold's house. Boswell, Reynolds and Garrick are seen in the back row sitting next to each other from left to right; with the unmistakeable figure of Dr Johnson holding the entire company enthralled with his conversation at the head of the table. Next to him sits Edmund Burke, then Burney and Oliver Goldsmith at the end of the table.

it was first built in 1326. **Robert Dudley**, Earl of Leicester, had virtually rebuilt it in 1563 before it passed, through marriage, to the Earl of Essex, hence its name. Amongst those who lived there were Nicholas Barbon, builder; Sir Orlando Bridgeman, Lord Keeper in Charles II's reign. For a time, in the following century, Charles Edward Stuart, the Young Pretender, lived there. Henry Fielding resided there for a time, as well as James Savage, the architect; Theophilius Lindsey, the Unitarian Minister and Dr Samuel Johnson, the lexicographer.

Dr Samuel Johnson (1709–1784) made this part of London his own, and no street in London is so linked to a single personality as Fleet Street is to the name of Dr Johnson. In the eighteenth century the street was narrow and cobbled, and until 1765, it had no pavements. Johnson, a heavy man, did not find his feet suited to so rough a surface. And, anyway, we are told, his walking manners were imperfect. Kearsly, the bookseller, who had often watched Johnson, described his gait as 'heavily headlong'. His gigantic head rolled forward, high above the heads of the Fleet Street crowd, 'followed by his huge body in concomitant and proportionate rhythm, while his feet appeared to have very little to do with his motion'. 'Sir, let us take a walk down Fleet Street', is a saying often attributed to Dr Johnson. In fact, the words are apocryphal. The quotation was imagined about Johnson by George Augustus Sala, who admitted: 'To the best of my knowledge and belief Dr Johnson never said a word about taking a walk down Fleet Street; but my innocent supercherie was, I fancy, implicitly believed in for at least a generation by the majority of magazine readers.' It was, and even Kipling included it in *Many Inventions*. It does not really matter as we know that Johnson certainly strolled daily in Fleet Street, and its immediate area, and was known by all who worked there. He worshipped frequently at St Clement Danes, and his pew was in the gallery.

In his book *Prayer and Meditation* he refers to his visits there, touchingly admitting that punctuality was never one of his virtues, not even on a Sunday. 'I went to church, came in at the first of the Psalms', he records for Sunday April 22 1764. Sometimes he did not make it before the Litany, while in April 1771, he records: 'Boswell came to go to church; we had tea, but I did not eat. Talk lost our time and we came to church late, at the second lesson.' In his later years Johnson became somewhat deaf, and would often leave his pew in the high gallery to be nearer the altar during the communion service. Johnson was a familiar figure to all who worshipped there. He was even better known at the Cheshire Cheese, in Wine Office Court, the historic inn off Fleet Street, which enjoys more associations with Johnson than any other public building in London. Johnson, his friend Dr Goldsmith, Sir Joshua Reynolds and Boswell made the Cheese, as it is known, their second home. 'Not the least delightful characteristic of the Cheese' wrote a customer, Thomas Reid, 'is the persistency of its old customers. Those who have once been admitted to its charmed circle soon become wedded to its ways and remain faithful.' By such terms, Dr Johnson's marriage to the Cheese was second to none. On one visit there, warmed and happy by the food and ale, he exclaimed to his company: 'There is nothing which has yet been contrived by man, by which so much happiness is produced as by a good tavern or inn.' Goldsmith lived nearly opposite the Cheese, at 6 Wine Office Court, and it was here that he wrote the *Vicar of Wakefield* which Johnson, after another such beneficial lunch, took with him to the publisher, old John Newbery, and sold for £60. At this time, Johnson was living in **17 Gough Square, EC4**, less than a minute's walk away, and he was a constant visitor at the Cheese, sometimes preferring to retire with his friends to a room upstairs to gorge himself and to deliver his thunderous

opinions. It was said of Johnson that while the Cheese was open nothing but a hurricane would induce him to cross Fleet Street in search of another hostelry. It is doubtful that the famous pudding, still served at the Cheese, a delicious dish of beefsteak, kidneys, oysters, mushrooms and other fascinating ingredients, was introduced to the menu by the time Johnson sat in his favourite chair, beneath a copy of a portrait by Reynolds. It is said that old William, the head waiter, was at the height of his glory on pudding days, considering it his duty to go round to the different tables insisting that the guests should have a second or even third helping. 'Any gentlemen say Pudden?' was his query. The crusty customer who growled back on one occasion, 'No gentleman says Pudden!' remains anonymous, and any way it failed to cure William's bad pronunciation. Dickens, Thackeray, Thomas Hood, Gladstone, Disraeli, or even Longfellow and Mark Twain, all became visitors at the Cheese to enjoy the same pleasures that had been taken by the great Dr Johnson. He died in 1784 and was buried in Westminster Abbey.

Fanny Burney (1752–1840) the authoress, lived at **11 Bolton Street, W1,** where she is commemorated by a plaque, and it is she who has left us one of the most graphic descriptions of Dr Johnson. The daughter of a Doctor of Music, she had already turned to writing by the time that Johnson called on the Burney household in 1777. She records in her diary: 'He is, indeed, very ill favoured; is tall and stout; but stoops terribly; he is almost bent double. His mouth is almost continually opening and shutting as if he was chewing. He has a strange method of frequently twirling his fingers and twisting his hands. His body is in continual agitation, seesawing up and down; his feet are never a moment quiet; and, in short, his whole person is in perpetual motion. His dress, too, considering the times, and that he had meant to put on his best becomes, being engaged to dine in a

large company, was as much out of the common road as his figure; he had a large wig, snuff-colour coat, and gold buttons, but no ruffles to his shirt, doughty [dirty] fists, and black worsted stockings. He is shockingly short sighted, and did not, till she held out her hand to him, even know Mrs Thrale.' Since Mrs Thrale was the lady who had brought Dr Johnson to the Burney household on that occasion, Fanny's feeling of a certain distaste towards the Doctor, for she was only aged 16 at the time, may be forgiven. But as soon as Johnson began to speak, Fanny was enraptured.

When, in 1778 the following year Fanny Burney published her first novel *Evelina* anonymously, Johnson, who was in on the secret, championed her authorship extravagantly even claiming that Fielding never wrote anything to equal it. He claimed further that 'Samuel Richardson would have been really afraid of her', and, while comparing her writing to Goldsmith's, said '*The Vicar of Wakefield* is very faulty; there is nothing of real life in it, and very little of nature. It is a mere fanciful performance'. Of course, Johnson was merely flattering the attractive young woman, who he insisted on sitting with whenever they happened to meet at dinner. Nevertheless, it is still true to say that Fanny Burney's racy, and biting reportage was enormously refreshing by contrast with the weightier literary style of the period, and Johnson, who loved gossip, read her avariciously. Her style appealed, too, to the circles about whom she wrote, and when her authorship of *Evelina* became public knowledge, she became immensely prominent. She reached as far as an appointment in Queen Charlotte's household where her charms sustained her position until ill health forced her to retire. In 1793, she married General D'Arblay, a French refugee in England, returning with him to France in 1802 only to be interned there by Napoleon until 1812. The last

Right: *H. G. Wells pictured in May 1940 at the age of 74.*
Left: *Hanover Terrace, seen from Regent's Park, the home of H. G. Wells and Ralph Vaughan Williams.*

part of her life was spent in England, at this residence in Bolton Street where she completed her literary memoirs.

William Pitt (1708–1778) Earl of Chatham, had residence for a time at **10 St James's Square, SW1,** where another Prime Minister Stanley, Earl of Derby(1799–1869)also lived. Another statesman, **Sir Robert Walpole** (1676–1745) is commemorated at **5 Arlington Street, SW1**. Pitt and Walpole held high office when political power was sustained not by democratic appeal but by influence and patronage. And also by sheer oratorical flair. Pitt, Lord Chesterfield wrote '... has very little parliamentary knowledge; his matter is generally flimsy, and his arguments often weak; but his eloquence is superior, his actions graceful, his enunciation just and harmonious; his periods are well turned, and every word he makes use of is the very best, and the most expressive that can be used in that place'. The battle for patronage was intense, calculated and vicious, and gossip was a ready weapon to be used whenever the right moment presented itself. The following farcical situation is told by Horace Walpole, about his father, Robert, who courting favour had turned his attentions to the wife of the future King of England. At the same time Lord Chesterfield, himself equally ambitious as a politician, and just as dependent on patronage, had turned his attentions to the future King's mistress. 'Lord Chesterfield', wrote Walpole, 'one Twelfth Night at Court had won so large a sum of money that he thought it imprudent to carry it home in the dark and deposited it with the mistress.' This late night visit turned out to be more imprudent still, for the meeting between Chesterfield and the future King's mistress was witnessed by the future Queen, whose own apartments overlooked the lighted window where the encounter was taking place. The next day, 'The [future] Queen inferred great intimacy, and thenceforward he [Chesterfield] could obtain no favour at Court; and

finding himself desperate went into Opposition. My father', writes Horace Walpole, 'had become the principal object of the peer's satirical wit, though not ... the mover of his disgrace.'

Lord Palmerston (1784–1865) commemorated at **100 Piccadilly** became Prime Minister years later. **Lord John Russell** (1792–1878) also Prime Minister and commemorated at **37 Chesham Place, SW1**, was one of several politicians who lived in close proximity to the Houses of Parliament, all of whom are commemorated by Blue Plaques: **Sir Henry Campbell-Bannerman** (1836–1908) **6 Grosvenor Place, W1; Lord Haldane,** statesman and philosopher (1856–1928) **Queen Anne's Gate, SW1; William Huskisson** (1770–1830) **28 St James's Place, SW1; Lord Rosebery,** (1847–1929) Prime Minister and first Chairman of The London County Council, **20 Charles Street, W1;** and **Stanley Baldwin** (1867–1947) Prime Minister, **93 Eaton Square, SW1**.

H. G. Wells (1866–1946) is commemorated at **13 Hanover Terrace, NW1** where he lived for the last ten years of his life. Wells, a short, compact man, inclined to plumpness, with grey and untidy hair is described as having eyes that were either meditative, or with an impish twinkle. He had little to smile about in the years of his residence at Hanover Terrace, which had previously been the home of Alfred Noyes, the poet. 'I am looking for a house to die in', Wells said to Noyes as he negotiated to take over the lease. He was also awaiting the grim inevitability of the Second World War which he had been predicting for so long. It is said by N. and J. Mackenzie in *The Time Traveller* that when Ford Madox Ford found himself at the front in the First World War, 'he noted that he had been so conditioned to modern warfare by reading the novels of Wells that when he actually experienced it he felt apathetic and resigned'. Whatever horrors Wells had imagined for his readers about the First World War, he was under no illusions that the next confrontation of world powers would

Left: *H. G. Wells' house at 13 Hanover Terrace, NW1.*
Below: *The entrance to Ralph Vaughan Williams's house at 10 Hanover Terrace, NW1.*

be an even bloodier conflict, with even more terrifying consequences for the human race. It had been after the First World War that Wells had started his assault on education, whose failures and shortcomings he had blamed for the ignorance of mankind, and the inevitability of war. But while the world read the books of H. G. Wells spellbound, they did not heed his warnings, and it was with a helpless horror that he saw the approach of 1939. The year before Wells moved to Hanover Terrace he had started work on a film screenplay of his book *Things to Come* for Alexander Korda. His work in films was to give him some relief from the depressing business of international conferences he felt it his duty to attend, which only confirmed his deep forebodings about the future of mankind. Wells enjoyed his trips abroad, but none more during this time than his visit to Hollywood, when he stayed with Charlie Chaplin, with whom he enjoyed an especially happy relationship. When war came Wells, then an old man, stood helplessly by. He continued to write in the large, elegant, book-lined drawing room at Hanover Terrace, occasionally rising in the middle of the night to put out incendiary bombs with the help of his two servants, but there was little pleasure in his work any more. The dropping of the first atomic bomb just a few months before his death in 1946 filled him with despair.

Ralph Vaughan Williams (1872–1958) the composer, who lived nearby at **10 Hanover Terrace, NW1**, was never so pessimistic in his last years. It was his custom, after attending a concert, and then a supper party with friends, to arrange with his chauffeur to be driven out at dawn into the depths of the English countryside where the ageing musician, sitting in the back of his car, and with a blanket wrapped around his legs for warmth, would unwind the window, and wait through the final hushed moments of departing darkness until the dawn chorus of birdsong began to break out all about him.

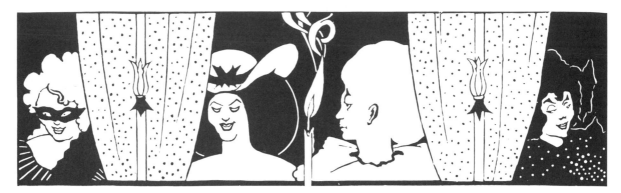

Then, refreshed, and at peace, he would instruct the chauffeur to turn the car back to London, and his sleep.

Admiral Earl Beatty and **Admiral Thomas Cochrane** are both commemorated at nearby **Hanover Lodge, Regent's Park, NW1,** and **Dame Marie Tempest,** the actress, is remembered at **24 Park Crescent, NW1.**

T. E. Lawrence (1888–1935) is commemorated at **14 Barton Street, SW1,** where he lived briefly after returning to England in 1922. It was after a dinner party encounter with Winston Churchill, who mentions the meeting in his book *Great Contemporaries*, that 'Lawrence of Arabia' was invited to join the Colonial Office. Whitehall was hardly to Lawrence's liking, and the appointment did not last.

Another brief link with London, this time a literary one, is sustained by the plaque at **6 Chesterfield Street, W1** where **W. Somerset Maugham** (1874–1965) is commemorated. Maugham's only indigenous London novel was his first one, *Liza of Lambeth*, written in 1895, when he was 21. He was then a fourth year medical student at St Thomas's Hospital, SE1, and had been working as an obstetric clerk in the Lambeth slums. The manuscript, Robin Maugham records in his book *Somerset and All The Maughams* was written 'in jerky and uncertain handwriting' in three exercise books bought in Paris. The original title of the book was *A Lambeth Idyll*, and Maugham had written on the flyleaf 'P.S. This novel, my first, was written in 1895 at 11 Vincent Square, Westminster'. The novel was a success, and so Maugham jettisoned his life as a doctor to become an author instead.

Aubrey Beardsley (1872–1898) the artist, lived for a time at **114 Cambridge Street, SW1.** His very short career, when he achieved almost instant success with the publication of his first book illustrations, was cut short by his death at the age of 26. His portraits, book plates, title pages and covers, including his work with Oscar Wilde on *The Yellow Book*, greatly influenced the decorative arts throughout Europe for generations to follow. The reverse cover design for *The Yellow Book* is shown above.

FURTHER NAMES COMMEMORATED IN WESTMINSTER

Mathew Arnold (1822–1888) poet and critic, lived at **2 Chester Square, SW1. Sir John Lubbock, Baron Avebury** (1834–1913) scientist and originator of the public bank holiday was born at **29 Eaton Place, SW1. Walter Bagehot** (1826–1877) the writer and banker, lived at **12 Upper Belgrave Street, SW1. George Basevi** (1794–1845) the architect who fell to an early death while inspecting the spire at Ely Cathedral, lived at **17 Savile Row, W1. Sir Francis Beaufort** (1774–1857) admiral and hydrographer, lived at **51 Manchester Street, W1.** The workshop of the cabinet makers **Thomas Chippendale** (1753–1813) and his son is commemorated at **61 St Martin's Lane, WC2. Thomas Cubitt** (1788–1855) master builder and the principal developer of Belgravia, lived at **3 Lyall Street, SW1. William Ewart** (1797–1869) reformer, lived at **16 Eaton Place, SW1. Sir Francis Galton** (1822–1911) explorer, statistician and founder of eugenics, lived at **42 Rutland Gate, SW7. Henry Gray** (1827–1861) the anatomist, lived at **8 Wilton Street, SW1. Henry Irving** (1838–1905) the actor, lived at **15a Grafton Street, W1. Cardinal Manning** (1808–1892) lived at **22 Carlisle Place, SW1. Prince Von Metternich** (1773–1858) Austrian statesman, stayed for a time at **44 Eaton Place, SW1. Florence Nightingale** (1820–1910) saviour of the wounded in the Crimean War, lived in a house on the site of **10 South Street, W1. Lord Raglan** (1788–1855) fated Commander in the Crimean War, and himself a victim of it, lived at **5 Stanhope Gate, W1. F. E. Smith** (1872–1930) Earl of Birkenhead, lawyer and statesman, lived at **32 Grosvenor Gardens, SW1. Charles Stanhope,** 3rd Earl (1753–1816) lived at **20 Mansfield Street, W1. Sir Richard Westmacott** (1775–1856) sculptor, lived and died at **14 South Audley Street, W1.**

Left: A self-portrait of Aubrey Beardsley shown alongside his back cover design for 'The Yellow Book'.

Henry Irving's residence in Grafton Street, W1, on the corner of Bond Street. Irving lived here during some of his most triumphant years on the West End stage.

Elizabeth Barrett Browning photographed at the age of 54, one year before her death in 1861.

ST MARYLEBONE

At **50 Wimpole Street, W1**, there is a commemorative plaque to **Elizabeth Barrett Browning** (1806–1861). She moved here after living with her family for a time at **99 Gloucester Place, W1**. Tennyson called Wimpole Street a 'long unlovely street', and E. Beresford Chancellor refers to the house as unlovely, too, 'owing to the maniacal selfishness of its owner', Elizabeth's father. The house where the Barretts of Wimpole Street lived has been rebuilt now, but even so the story of Elizabeth's romance with Robert Browning is as fresh and romantic today as it was when news of it broke on an admiring London society. The story is of absorbing interest, not only of the characters of the lovers themselves – their geniuses and their ardent natures – but because of the peculiar circumstances involved, which showed Browning as a man of exceptional devotion, and Elizabeth Barrett as a woman of unusual trust. There was also a third character involved, that of the father, simply a cruel, tyrannical autocrat, who claimed sole control of his children's destinies, and who had an objection, amounting almost to insanity, on the subject of their marriage.

Elizabeth herself was an invalid. She had fallen from her horse in childhood, and suffered severe spinal trouble. Often, she had to be carried from her bed to her sofa, and only rarely was she well enough to reach her sitting room unaided. She was retiring and shy, and preferred to avoid seeing people. 'There is nothing to see in me, nor to hear in me' she wrote to Robert Browning when he begged to visit her. 'If my poetry is worth anything to any eye, it is the flower of me . . . it had all my colours; the rest of me is nothing but a root, fit

for the ground and dark.' Nevertheless, in May 1845, Browning achieved his wish. They knew each other already through their works. Elizabeth's poems were vigorous, large-hearted, teeming with richness and imagery. They appealed strongly to Browning. She thought highly of his poems, too. In her *Lady Geraldine's Courtship* she makes her hero read to his ladylove from Browning's volume called *Bells and Pomegranates*. Between many writers, such mutual admiration could merely exist on a literary level. Between Browning and Elizabeth, however, a much deeper closeness was established because they were speaking to each other on more than just poetic terms. Browning at this time was aged 36, and already well known. He was slim, dark, his hair 'purply black', and very handsome. Macready the actor had written of him a little earlier 'He looks and speaks more like a young poet than any one I have ever seen'. Elizabeth was six years older, though young looking for her years. Her pale face was framed in dark curls, making it look – to use one of her own phrases in *Aurora Leigh*, 'like a point of moonlit water down a well'. Her eyes were her most striking feature – Browning confesses that when he met her first he saw only her eyes – they were wonderfully expressive. All her personality was vivid and eager, and there was an exquisite daintiness in her poise.

They met in her sick room, and Elizabeth received him lying on her sofa. He was still ignorant of the injury she had, as well as the prejudices of her father. He wrote to her, telling her of his love. Elizabeth sent the letter back again asking him to burn it. Her father, she knew, would never approve of it, still less of her marriage. 'He would rather see me dead at his feet than yield the point', she wrote. But Browning refused to be thwarted by such arbitrary considerations. He persisted with his attentions and devotions, until Elizabeth capitulated. The wooing had to be secret, the

engagement secret; for had Browning's intentions been guessed, Mr Barrett would have forbidden all communication. The meetings had to be carefully planned, skilfully contrived, and often postponed – though in a good week the lovers managed to meet three times. Only Elizabeth's sisters knew of the affaire, and helped in every way that they could, though, such was the hawk-like way in which their father watched over their every move, they were of little real assistance in solving Elizabeth's and Browning's central dilemma – how to marry without being obstructed by the spiteful rage and possessiveness of her father. Their break came when the doctors pronounced that a visit to Italy was essential for Elizabeth's health. Predictably, Mr Barrett refused to contemplate such a trip. Friends offered to accompany Elizabeth; those who were strong enough argued her case with her father. He remained obdurate. Browning, of everyone who insisted she should go, was the most passionate, the most fervent, and Elizabeth, realising that such an opportunity for escape would not present itself again, put herself wholly in his hands. Browning told her that an immediate and secret marriage was the only possible course to take.

On the day when she had to make her final decision, she hired a carriage and with her sister drove to Regent's Park. She got out, walked on the grass, and stood for a moment leaning against a tree looking at the sky. It was many years since she had felt the ground beneath her feet, and the open air about her. Then she drove home again, and having tested her strength in such a way, she gave her consent to the elopement.

The Wimpole Street romance has the kind of ending best-selling writers hope to contrive in their stories. On September 12 1846, Elizabeth walked quietly out of the house, and married Robert Browning in Marylebone Church. Then she returned home as if nothing had happened.

From then until the day of her elopement, a period of seven days, she and her husband did not meet. Browning could not bring himself to go to the house in Wimpole Street and ask for her at the door by her maiden name. Then, in the late afternoon of September 19, accompanied by her maid and her dog, Flush, Mrs Browning stole from her father's house. The family was at dinner; Flush was only just prevented from barking. That night she and her husband took the boat to Le Havre, and went on their way to Paris. In time they went on to live at Pisa and Florence, where their home Casa Guidi still stands opposite the Pitti Palace.

Mrs Elizabeth Browning died in 1861. Browning himself returned to London, and lived for 25 years at 19 Warwick Gardens W2, overlooking the Paddington Canal, before moving to **De Vere Gardens, W8**, where his stay there is commemorated by a plaque. He was visiting his son in Venice in December 1899, staying in the Palazzio Rezzonico, when he died on the very day that his last book of verse was published back in his native country. The plaque in Wimpole Street was erected in 1937.

A hundred years before Browning's romance with Elizabeth Browning, St Marylebone was still on the edge of open country, and footpads, thieves and highwaymen abounded, and no more than in the notorious area of Marylebone Fields. Such men were so deft in action, and so swift of foot that few, if any, were ever caught, so it is unlikely that they ever occupied the cells in Marylebone Watch House, beneath the room lived in by the local Beadle. Those locked in the cells for the night and left to sober up were more likely to be the local drunks, one of whom, **James Boswell** (1740–1795) is commemorated by a plaque at **122 Great Portland Street, W1**. It may seem unfair to Boswell to introduce his name in this way, but the fact remains that at the end of his life, much of which anyway had been dedicated to good

Left: *Joshua Reynolds sketch of Boswell. It is signed for Reynolds by Boswell, 'your faithful and affectionate and humble servant, James Boswell'.*
Below: *In this caricature by Rowlandson, Boswell (centre) is seen taking refreshment at night with Dr Johnson. The boredom of Dr Johnson, and the barely concealed weariness of the waiter in the background suggest that Boswell and his enraptured lady friend have been monopolising the evening's conversation.*

enjoyment, with his wife and his great friend and stimulant Dr Johnson both dead, Boswell drank not just excessively, but recklessly. An anonymous contemporary of Boswell's is quoted by C. E. Vulliamy as writing: 'In the last years of his life Boswell still continued to frequent the societies which he had been wont to delight. But death carried away, one after another, many of his dearest companions . . . his jokes, his song, his sprightly effusions of wit and wisdom were ready, but did not appear to possess upon all occasions their wonted power of enlivening the social lot . . . his fits of dejection became more frequent, and of longer duration. Convivial society became continuously more necessary to him, while his power of enchantment over it continued to decline. Even the excitement of deep drinking every evening became often desirable to raise his spirits above melancholy depression.'

Carlyle was even more direct about Boswell during his time in Great Portland Street, which were also the last five years of his life. 'Boswell', he wrote, 'was a wine bibber, and gross liver; gluttonously fond of whatever would yield him a little solacement . . . vain, heedless, a babbler . . .' In fact, Boswell at this time was more than a babbler. He was an incoherent, raucous drunkard, and life must have contained but few pleasures for the brave daughter who was looking after him. One night he failed to come home at all, having been locked up in the cells of the watch house by the Beadle for 'crying in the streets'. Boswell had been weaving home after a heavy session when he passed the local watchman. It was two o'clock, and the watchman was issuing forth his usual cry 'Past two o'clock and all's well' when suddenly he heard Boswell swelling the chorus as he lumbered off in the other direction. Annoyed at this interference with his duties, as well as being worried by Boswell's unmelodious disturbance of the peace, the famous writer was wheeled briskly down to the watch house, and

pitched promptly into a cell. Boswell's defence the next morning was that he was trying to teach the watchman the correct inflection for his cry. With characteristic lawyer's cunning, he explained to the Beadle that if the emphasis of the cry was placed on the word 'past' rather than on the hour that was subsequently being announced, then no one could possibly be expected to understand what time it was. Raw tempered though he may have been after such a disturbed night, the Beadle was forced to admit that Boswell had satisfied the charge, and he was allowed to return home, doubtless to another shouting match, this time with his daughter. Carlyle, however, shall have the last word on Boswell, as he said, to redress the balance of his previous words: '. . . on the other hand, what great and genuine good lay in him was no wise so evident . . . the man had an open sense, an open loving heart which so few have.' Boswell died here on May 19 1795.

Two more lawyers are commemorated in Manchester Square, both of them politicians. At **20 Cavendish Square, W1, Lord Asquith** (1852–1928) lived, while the house at **5 Cavendish Square** commemorates the residence of **Quintin Hogg** (1845–1903) the social reformer and founder of the London Polytechnic. Asquith moved here following his marriage to Margot Tennant. He was at the time Home Secretary, and was to become Prime Minister for eight years from 1908–1916. Though he lived for much of this period in Downing Street, he kept on with his house in Cavendish Square, not selling it until 1919.

History, it might be said, is a matter for politicians, while the mysteries of politics should be left to historians. Certainly **Henry Hallam** (1777–1859) commemorated at **67 Wimpole Street, W1** had much to wrestle with as he wrote his mighty *Constitutional History Of England From The Accession Of Henry VII To The Death Of George II* at this house. The title itself is daunting enough. Hallam, however, won the admiration of his contemporaries not only for his scholarship, but for the way he achieved it in the face of great personal tragedies. He lived in this house from 1819 to 1840. His son, aged 22 had been a great friend of Tennyson's at Cambridge. In 1833, Arthur Hallam died quite suddenly while travelling on the Continent, and in that year Tennyson began his *In Memoriam* to express his grief for his lost friend. It is from the opening lines of this poem that we get a direct reference to this house:

'Dark House, by which once more I stand
Here in the long unlovely street
Doors, where my heart was used to beat
So quickly waiting for the hand,
A hand that can be clasped no more . .'

Henry Hallam was desolated by the loss of his son, but his grief continued when in 1837, his daughter Ellen died, followed by his wife's death just three years later. The plaque was erected in 1904.

Another historian commemorated is **John Richard Green** (1837–1883) who lived at **4 Beaumont Street, WC1**. Though Green lived a very much shorter life than Hallam, dying before he was 50, it was at least a less sombre one. In 1865, at the age of 28, Green was appointed vicar of St Philip's, in Stepney. But four years later he moved to Beaumont Street having been appointed librarian at Lambeth Palace. He also left Stepney, and the hectic life of a parish, in his own words 'to woo poverty and freedom', in other words to seek his fortune as a writer. Shortly after moving in he wrote to a friend: 'I hardly know yet whether I am on my head or my heels. It is so odd to be without a parish, without a parsonage, without a hundred bothers, interruptions, quarrels, questions to decide, engagements to recollect . . .' But he was already enjoying '. . . the cleaner streets, and above all my morning trot through the park. It is such a change too to get a chat when one likes, to be able to get a peep at good pictures, and to have one's mind free for the

things one cares about!' So much, one might be tempted to add, for Green's vocation as a Minister! The truth was, of course, that his real talents were as writer about history. He had left Oxford in 1860 with precisely that intention in mind, specifically, in fact, to write a history of the Archbishops of Canterbury. Though, as he has already testified, there was not much time for scholarship in a busy East End parish, Green's time in Stepney had been far from wasted. His wife, Alice Green, writing the introduction to the later editions of his famed, and immensely popular *Short History of the English People*, written during his time here at Beaumont Street, rightly observes: 'Books were not his only source of knowledge. To the last he looked on his London life as having given him the best lessons in history. It was with his churchwardens, his schoolmasters, in vestry meetings, in police courts, at boards of guardians, in service in chapel or church, in the daily life of the dock labourer, the tradesman, the costermonger, in the summer visitation of cholera, in the winter misery that followed economic changes, that he learnt what the life of the people meant as perhaps no historian had ever learnt it before.' Writing his *Short History* was hard, exhausting work. 'I do some bit of work every day' Green wrote from Beaumont Street in a letter to a friend. 'But work is very hard when one is weak and disheartened. Moreover, I have put a great deal of work into what I have done and have rewritten it again and again to get it to my liking.' Green was not a strong man. When Trinity College, Cambridge, offered him a lectureship in history, he declined it, saying, 'My winters abroad make it impossible for me'. He needed those months of softer air to recuperate. At length, in 1874, his *Short History* was published. It was an immediate success, exactly what it deserved. Mandell Creighton said: 'What Macaulay has done for a period of history, Green did for it as a whole.' Writing

Right: *From his house in Finchley Road, Thomas Hood could look across to Lord's Cricket Ground in the distance, and sometimes, while hard at work on a manuscript he viewed the activities of the cricketers at play with great envy.*

this work was not, however, without its lighter moments. In 1872, Green had invited a pre-Raphaelite friend to stay with him at his rooms. Green reconstructs the scene that greeted his eyes on his return to Beaumont Street where his creative friend had been so active in his absence: 'The doors are in the sea sickness style, green picked out with sickly blue! My poor writing desk, dear from many an association, had been clothed in light blue with lines of red. When I re-entered my rooms for the first time my artist friend had just begun covering it with black dragons. I "yowled", and dashed the paint boxes downstairs, but the dragons had already been completed, and yawn on me whenever I want to write a gay little note. "Is it nice?" I ask my landlady, sarcastic. That venerable woman stood gazing on the scene. "Not nice" replied the critic of the kitchen. "Not nice, sir, No! But certainly spruce!"' Green left this house in 1876, for Connaught Street. Later in his life he was on the move again, for the last time, to Kensington Square, with a loving wife to share the last few brief years of his life. He died in 1883, much loved and respected.

Thomas Hood (1799–1845) commemorated at **Devonshire Lodge, 28 Finchley Road, NW3**, was also held in affection and esteem by his friends. He also died young, aged 45. Hood spent the last two years of his life in this house, having moved here from nearby Elm Tree Road, where he had lived for the previous three years, at No. 17. The room where he worked here gave him a clear view of Lord's Cricket Ground. He complained humorously about this, saying how unfair it was that 'when he was at work, he could see others at play'. Hood was a popular writer. He was a Londoner, born above his father's bookshop in the Poultry in the City. By the time he was 23, he was sub-editor on the *London Magazine*. Twenty years later he was to be editing his own magazine *Hood's Magazine* from 1 Adam Street, WC2. Miss Mary Balmanno

wrote 'in outward appearance Hood conveyed the idea of a clergyman. His figure was slight and invariably dressed in black, his face pallid; the complexion delicate, and features regular . . .'. But there was nothing dull about Hood. He had a warm, and subtle sense of humour, which he used to much effect in his writing. Like his close friend Charles Dickens he was sickened by the black misery of the slums, and delighted in writing evocatively about the misery of the lowly paid, knowing perfectly well that his neat turn of phrase would cause anguish and guilt in the minds of his middle class readers. He was a skilful and careful enough writer, however, not to offend. Douglas Jerrold – a fellow contributor to *Punch* – wrote of him: 'His various pens touched alike the springs of laughter and the source of tears.' More and more of his time was spent in bed. It was only with great difficulty, and one must think, courage, that he hauled himself out of his sick bed one evening in 1842 to go down to Greenwich to attend a dinner on Dickens' return from America. There were many celebrities there, and all were delighted to see their popular friend in their midst once again. So much so that everyone at the dinner had wished to shake his hand. 'Very gratifying, wasn't it', Hood wrote a few days later in a letter to a friend, adding that his wife 'wants me to have that hand chopped off, bottled and preserved in spirits!'

In all probability, he would have travelled back from Greenwich in the same carriage as Dickens, who, by this time had moved from Doughty Street, and was living in nearby Devonshire Terrace, W1. Dickens came to see Hood several times on his sick bed, on one occasion bringing Longfellow with him. All this while Hood was being looked after by his wife. 'Mrs Hood', Mary Balmanno tells us, 'was a most amicable woman, of excellent manners and full of sincerity and goodness. She perfectly adored her husband, tending him like a

child, whilst he, with unbounded affection, seemed to delight to yield himself to her guidance. Nevertheless, true to his humorous nature, he loved to tease her with jokes and whimsical accusations, which were only responded to by ''Hood, Hood, how can you run on so?'' By the following year, 1843, the Hoods had moved to Devonshire Lodge. By now Hood was addressing letters headed 'From my Bed'. From his bedroom here, he wrote his *Drop of Gin* poem for *Punch*, followed by the even greater poem *The Song of The Shirt*. 'Now mind, Hood, mark my words', said Mrs Hood as she assembled the manuscript together for the post 'this will tell wonderfully. It is one of the best things you ever did.' The results justified her opinion. The poem appeared in the Christmas number of *Punch* that year, trebling the magazine's circulation. Now very ill, he remained full of typical good humour. 'I must remain' he quipped 'a lively Hood to get a livelihood', and, while his wife was trying to put on a poultice on his emaciated body, he observed with a sad smile, 'It seems a great deal of mustard for such a little meat'! To Thackeray he wrote in 1844, 'King death will claim me 'ere many months elapse. However, there's a good time coming, if not in this world, most assuredly in the next'. He had to refuse an invitation to go to a meeting with the brief dismissal 'For me all journeys are over save one'. Although he had been told by the doctors not to work he continued to do so, for, as he explained to Lord Lytton 'and so it will be to the end. I must die in harness. Like a hero – or a horse'. He died in 1845, and the plaque to him was erected in 1912.

Benjamin Haydon (1786–1846) the painter, commemorated at **116 Lisson Grove, NW1**, who died a year later than Hood, was a very different personality, and was singularly lacking in all the characteristics that made Hood so popular. Haydon, like Reynolds, was a native of Plymouth. After living for a time in central London, he had settled here in Lisson Grove for the fresh air and the good painting light. It would be wrong to say that Haydon was universally unpopular – he wasn't. He simply lacked tact and finesse, finding it easier to be abrasive, even rather ebullient towards his circle of acquaintances, and his fellow artists in particular. He had a volcanic temper, and an almost sadistic delight in proving others wrong – especially those who did not like his paintings. Once, in 1820, during the five years that he was living at Lisson Grove, he hired the Great Room in The Egyptian Hall in Piccadilly, for the duration of a whole year, to exhibit his monumental painting 'Christ's Entry In Jerusalem'. The point of this expensive exercise was not simply to show off his work – a natural enough thing for any artist to want to do – but to demonstrate the popularity of his work to the Academicians, with whom he was pursuing a long term quarrel about the principles of 'high art'. Haydon was constantly in debt, but despite the kindness of friends, and the assistance of patrons, he was unable to come to terms with himself and his talents. The patrons fell away, the gifts of money stopped. He persisted in the arrogant belief that the world owed him a living, spongeing off banks, bullying people into buying his pictures. Finally, it all stopped. In June 1846, he had put a large historical picture on display. Everyone had come to see it. No one had bought it. In a rage of spite and self-pity he scrawled the words 'God Forgive Me' in his diary, and killed himself in front of the painting. **Charles Rossi**, the sculptor, and his friend, who shared this house with him for a time, is commemorated at the same address.

Thomas Huxley (1825–1895) the biologist, commemorated at **38 Marlborough Place, NW8**, displayed no such volatile characteristics. He came near to anger on moving into this house, however, in 1872. In a letter to Tyndall, his friend, he writes: 'Getting into it was an awful job, made worse than needful by the infamous weather we have had for weeks and months, and by the stupid delays of the workmen, whom we had fairly to shove out as we came in. We are settling down by degrees, and shall be very comfortable by and by, though I do not suppose that we shall be able to use the drawing room for two or three months to come.' His son Leonard, writing about the house in *The Life and Letters of T. H. Huxley*, described it as, 'on the north side of that quiet street... The irregular front of the house ... distinguished only by its extremely large windows was screened from the road by a high oak paling, and a well grown row of young lime trees. Taken as a whole it was not without character, and certainly unlike most London houses it was certainly built for comfort, designed within stringent limits as to cost, to give each member of the family room to get away by himself or herself is disposed ... a small garden lay in front of the house, a considerably larger garden behind, wherein the chief ornament was a large apple tree.' The Huxleys were a musical family, and a musical evening was a highlight of their social calendar. High tea would be over by 6.30 p.m., after which the Huxley daughters sang to the assembled company. One gains the impression of an atmosphere of solemnity, even reverence at these occasions, for poetry was not permitted by Huxley inside the drawing room, being considered vulgar. It is recorded, though, that on one occasion, Henry Irving, a guest at one of these parties, successfully got away with a rendering of *The Dream of Eugene Aram*.

Huxley was an extremely busy man, lecturing at South Kensington, where he was the staunchest supporter of the theories of his friend Darwin which were faced with a great deal of stubborn, and stupid Victorian prejudice. In 1873, while he was convalescing from an illness, he received a most pleasant surprise from Darwin, who wrote to inform him that a group of friends had contributed the sum of £2000 to Huxley so that he could get away for a while and recuperate. It was a kind and generous gesture, and one which Huxley received gratefully, spending several months on the Continent. His health finally broke in 1884, when he resigned himself to a life of retirement. He finished his lectures at South Kensington, where, amongst others, he was teaching a young H. G. Wells; and gave up such other duties as the Presidency of the Royal Society, and being ex-officio Trustee of the British Museum. His last years were spent in Eastbourne. **Sir Ambrose Fleming** (1849–1945) the scientist and electrical engineer is commemorated at **9 Clifton Gardens, NW8**.

It was to the Royal Society that **Michael Faraday** (1791–1867) commemorated by a plaque at **48 Blandford Street, W1**, read a paper about magneto-electric induction, in 1831. The event was memorable enough, for the systems Faraday was investigating were effectively the forerunner of modern electricity. More startling, perhaps, was how a man of such humble origins had risen so swiftly to a position of such eminence in the scientific world. Faraday's father was a blacksmith with rooms in Jacob Well Mews, W1. A few yards away was a bookshop kept by George Riebau, where, in 1804, aged 13, Faraday started as an errand boy. The following year Riebau apprenticed Faraday as a bookbinder and bookseller for a period of seven years. They were to be the most formative years of Faraday's life, and Riebau's bookshop became, effectively, Faraday's university. Before long he was also attending evening classes, and the direction of his eventual career was firmly sealed when, a few years later, he was taken on by Sir Humphry Davy, as a laboratory assistant. The plaque was erected here by the Royal Society of Arts in 1876.

Books and science come together, too at **3 Manchester Square, W1**, where **John Hughlings Jackson**, is commemorated. Jackson, a physician, was the first man to study systematically

Right: *This elegant plaque at 2 Manchester Square, W1 to Sir Julius Benedict was erected by the London County Council in 1934. The house, like most of the others in Manchester Square, is now in use commercially. It is interesting to note that Manchester Square itself is private property, protected by the Manchester Square Act which has never been repealed.*
Left: *The home of John Hughlings Jackson, the physician, in Manchester Square, W1. The railings on the right are the frontage of Sir Julius Benedict's house, at No. 2.*

the localisation of the brain functions, and in so doing he discovered the causes, and then found the cures for many nervous diseases. Dr Raymond Crawford, writing on behalf of the Royal College of Physicians, in 1930, claiming a plaque for Jackson wrote: '...one of his greatest discoveries was the proof that certain portions of the brain controlled the voluntary movements of the body, and that diseases of this part caused fits and paralysis.' Tragically, his wife, Elizabeth, whom he had married in 1876, died after a short illness of thrombosis of the cerebral veins, precisely associated with local convulsions of the type Jackson was then investigating. Jackson was a quiet man, not fond of public functions. He preferred to dip into Dickens, or his beloved Samuel Johnson, whom he could quote at length. In Manchester Square also lived **Sir Julius Benedict**, the musician, commemorated at No. 2, and **Lord Alfred Milner**, the statesman, remembered at No. 14.

Captain Frederick Marryat the novelist, lived at **3 Spanish Place, W1**. Born in Westminster in 1792, he went to sea at 14, and did not return to live in England until 1832. It was not until ten years later that he came to Spanish Place, where he wrote *Masterman Ready*. 'It was here' wrote his daughter, Mrs Church, 'in the tiniest of houses, furnished according to his own taste, a very gem in its adornment that he received the visitors who made the little rooms brilliant with their conversation and wit.' Marryat was a short, stout, thick set man, who walked 'and looked and spoke as if he were at home only on the quarter deck.' There must have been times when the publishers of his novels wished that Marryat had stayed at sea, and had never taken up writing, for 'his handwriting was so minute that the compositor having given up the task of deciphering it in despair, the copyist had to stick a pin in at the place where he had left off to ensure his finding it again when he resumed his task.' Marryat died in 1848. This plaque was erected in 1953, and he shares it with **George**

Grossmith (junior) (1847–1935) the actor manager, who was born the year after his death.

George Grossmith (senior) (1847–1912) the actor author, is commemorated at **28 Dorset Square, NW1**. Two other theatrical names remembered in St Marylebone are **Sir Arthur Pinero** (1855–1934) the playwright, who lived at **115a Harley Street, W1** and **Sir Charles Wyndham** (1837–1919) the actor manager, at **43 York Terrace, NW1**.

The plaque to **Joseph Nollekens** (1737–1823) the sculptor, at **44 Mortimer Street, W1**, commemorates not only a fine craftsman, but reminds us also of a man of extreme meanness and avarice. Born without means he had ammassed a fortune of over £300,000 by the time he died 86 years later simply by hoarding almost every penny he ever earned. His fees were unusually high. For his bust of Pitt he received the huge sum of £4000. Considering therefore, the size, and reliability of his income, his lifestyle was simply amazing. To his fellow artists, his miserly behaviour was legendary. He imposed a sordid economy on his wife. Wilmot Harrison recounts that 'a couple of mould candles were made to serve by careful management through the winter, being never lighted until late in the evening, unless a visitor called, and then they would wait until they heard a second rasp at the door lest the first should have been a runaway, and the candle wasted'. In Nollekens' studio, J. T. Smith mentions in his superbly anecdotal book *Nollekens and His Times* that he 'hung two bits of slate dangling upon a nail, on which Mr and Mrs Nollekens kept their separate memoranda of the day's expenditure; for they kept separate accounts against each other, as to letters, porters employed or things purchased for the house'. These 'things' were very few and far between. For years two pieces of old green canvas were festooned at the lower parts of windows as blinds, and, on the rare occasions when any new furniture entered the house, visitors were only allowed a quick peep at it by

Left: *The home of Captain Frederick Marryat and George Grossmith in Spanish Place, one of the few examples of houses in London which are marked by more than one Blue Plaque.*

Mrs Nollekens lest the upholstery be spoilt, or the woodwork scratched. The habit of Nollekens and his wife at table can only be described as parsimonious. A single loaf of bread was made to last a week and a visit to a friend's house offered a timely opportunity for a little hoarding. The yearly sight, at the Royal Academy Banquet, of Nollekens stealing the nutmegs from the table when he supposed nobody else was looking, was always an occasion of great mirth relished by his fellow artists! Nollekens, a tiny, bow-legged man, with a big head and a nose like an eagle's beak contrasted strangely with his much larger wife who, says Wilmot Harrison 'stood a good head and shoulders above her short thick set husband'. Mrs Nollekens was no less seduced by wealth than her husband, and kept, in the library, a hoard of 1100 guineas. Although paper money had already been introduced to the economy, the system was not trusted by Mrs Nollekens. 'These guineas she would look over pretty often', Smith tells us, 'and weigh in her hands against each other, partly for the enjoyment she felt in counting her wealth, and partly to discover if anyone had been deceiving her with short coin or wealth.' Yet, despite their habits, they were held in much affection by their neighbours.

Another eccentric commemorated nearby is **Henry Fuseli** (1741–1825) the artist who lived at **37 Foley Street, W1.** Fuseli, was a Swiss and Professor of Painting at the Royal Academy. Benjamin Haydon, then a youth aged 18, visited Fuseli's rooms shortly after his arrival in London. Haydon recalled the occasion in his autobiography: 'I followed her (the maid servant) into a gallery or show room ... I heard his footstep, and fancied Fuseli himself to be a giant ... and saw a little boy's hand slide round the edge of the door, followed by a little white headed, thin faced man in an old flannel dressing gown tied round his waist with a piece of rope, and upon his head the bottom of Mrs

Fuseli's work basket ... All apprehension vanished on his saying ... in the mildest and kindest way, "Well, Mr Haydon, I have heard a great deal of you from Mr Hoare. Where are your drawings?" '

Such an oddity would have been appreciated by **Edward Lear** (1812–1888) who is remembered at **30 Seymour Street, W1.** Lear has only slight links with St Marylebone. He lived in the area as a young man, needing somewhere close to the Regent's Park Zoo, where he had a commission from the Royal Zoological Society to do some drawings of parrots. Lear, shy, retiring, an epileptic, already an outsider looking in, presented an outstanding portfolio to the Zoo authorities, perfectly capturing the quirky individualism that makes the parrot such a subtle and fascinating bird. The portfolio was a success, and helped launch Lear, giving him the money and the confidence to travel. Some years later, in 1850, after being ten years in Italy, Greece and the Mediterranean Islands, Lear took a studio at 17 Stratford Place, off Oxford Street. The plaque was erected in 1960.

Also in **Seymour Street, W1** at **No. 12, Michael Balfe** (1808–1870) the composer is remembered. Balfe, an Irishman, came to London as a boy of 15 years in 1823. He was then a singer, and it was twenty years before he scored his big success after writing *The Bohemian Girl.* The show made him wealthy, and, in 1864, after living here for three years, he retired to the country, buying up a property in Hertfordshire, at Rowney Abbey, where he lived the life of a gentleman farmer. The plaque was erected in 1912.

Another musician, the much more famous French composer **Hector Berlioz** (1803–1869) is remembered for a short stay in Marylebone by a plaque at **58 Queen Anne Street, W1.** In the middle of the nineteenth century, Hector Berlioz made a number of trips to London, fulfilling professional engagements. He never maintained a household as such. Amongst other

Below: *The home of Edward Lear, which is now a hotel. Lear's old home in Seymour Street is twenty minutes walk from the Zoological Gardens in Regent's Park where he did much of his drawings.*
Far right: *A far cry from the cloistered precinct of Barchester, Anthony Trollope's old home in Montague Square still looks out amongst refined and dignified surroundings.*
Right: *Anthony Trollope painted by S. Laurence, when the writer was fifty years old.*

musicians, **Sir Charles Santley**, singer, who lived from 1834–1922, is remembered by a plaque at **13 Blenheim Road, NW8**, and **Charles Wesley** (1703–1788), the hymn writer and Divine, who lived here with his two sons is remembered at **1 Wheatley Street, W1**.

Lord Lister (1827–1912) who made such outstanding contributions to modern surgery, is remembered at **12 Park Crescent, W1**. It was while he was occupying the Chair at Glasgow University that he developed the theory that the great mortality rate which accompanied operations was due, not so much to the lack of surgical technique, but to the amount of germs applied to the wounds in the course of the operation. An eminent practitioner himself, he began specialising in developing and perfecting the guarantees of antiseptic surgery. He moved to this house in 1877 on his appointment to the Chair at King's College Hospital where he was once more engaged in clinical surgery – and where he began to test the validity of the principles of antiseptic treatment he had originated in Glasgow. He was a ceaseless worker, often being helped in his experiments by Mrs Lister. A medical colleague, Dr Stewart, called on him one afternoon to find 'him in his short sleeves, perspiring as usual, busy getting in order the exhibits for his lecture ... Mrs Lister was helping, also his nephew ... there was a large number of glasses and tubes ... we drove from his house to the lecture in Somerset House'. The plaque was erected only three years after his death in 1912.

Anthony Trollope (1815–1882) the novelist, commemorated at **39 Montague Square, W1**, would have admired the brisk, clinical fastidiousness which Lister displayed in his laboratory. Trollope, too, measured in exact, and precise terms the time which he would allow for work, and the time he would allow for play. 'I have never been a slave to this work' he wrote about his novels 'giving time, if not more than due time, to the amusements I have loved'. Even so, he

Right: Samuel Morse, here drawn after a photograph which shows him sitting beside his code transmitting device, which was named after him, would have been amused that the skyline outside his old home in London is now dominated by the giant Post Office Tower, one of the largest communications centres in Western Europe.

was a disciplined writer. 'Three hours a day', he declared, 'will produce as much as a man ought to write. It is still my custom to write with my watch before me, and to require myself 250 words every quarter of an hour.' This was no idle boast, as his obituary in *The Times* testified: 'As a rule, he rose early and worked till 11. Then, at the stroke of the clock, the pen was laid down, however lightly it might be turning off the sentences or though it might be working up to the climax of a sensational scene.' After that he was free to relax, and take his pleasures. Woe betide the nuisance, however, who may have interrupted him at his desk. One day, his thoughts were unsettled by a band of street musicians strumming and singing outside. Trollope, red in the face with anger, stood on his doorstep bellowing at them until they lowered their instruments and slouched dejectedly around the nearest corner. Had they only known, after 11 o'clock, but a few minutes later, they could have made as much noise as they liked! Trollope's chief recreation was to ride with the hounds, but when he was in London he entertained a great deal, as well as playing whist daily at the Garrick Club between tea and supper. Trollope was nearly 60 when he settled here, and it was only now that any great success came to him as a writer. As recently as 1867, only six years before his residence commenced in this house, he had still been working as an Inspector with the General Post Office, whose employment he had entered as a lowly clerk nearly 35 years before that. Trollope had left Winchester 'unable to work an ordinary sum or write a decent hand'. Some beginning for the eventual author of *Barchester Towers*! He travelled a great deal during his eight years at this house, visiting South Africa in 1877, and Iceland, the year after. An anonymous friend has left us the following brief glimpse of the man: 'It would be impossible to imagine anything less like his works than the author of them. The books are

full of gentleness, grace and refinement, the writer of them bluff, loud, stormy and contentious – neither a brilliant talker nor a good speaker, but a kinder hearted man and a truer friend never lived.' Trollope died in 1882. This plaque was erected in 1912.

From a figure such as Trollope who was so quintessentially English, time to mention, in contrast, **John Godley** (1814–1861) the founder of New Zealand, who is commemorated very close by Trollope's house at **48 Gloucester Place, W1**; **José de San Martin** (1778–1850), (The Liberator), Argentine soldier and statesman, who is remembered for a stay at **23 Park Road, NW1**; **Mustapha Reschid Pasha** (1800–1858) the Turkish statesman and reformer, at **1 Bryanston Square, NW1**, and **Field Marshal Lord Roberts**, at **47 Portland Place, W1**.

Samuel Morse, inventor of the Morse Code, is remembered at **141 Cleveland Street, W1**. He came from America to London in 1811, then aged 20, seeking his fame not as a scientist but as a painter. It was fortunate that Benjamin West, a fellow countryman, was then President of the Royal Academy, and supremo of the artistic establishment. Hearing that Morse was in London, West encouraged him in every way possible, making the right introductions, and also arranging for Morse to exhibit in the right places. In consequence, Morse's four years in London were a considerable success. Some aspects of London life he did not enjoy, however, especially the street cries. Writing to a friend he said: 'The cries of London are very annoying to me. I don't know how many times I have run to the windows expecting to see some poor creature in the agonies of death, but found, to my surprise, that it was only an old woman crying "Fardin Apples", or something of the kind.' Had Morse understood the language of Londoners better he would have realised that the old woman was merely quoting the price for her fruit, and had not discovered some delicious new brand name of apple. Perhaps he was conscious of such elementary

This unimposing terrace house in what was then a lowly area of London is typical of the sort of dwelling to which students like the young Tom Moore came in the late eighteenth century.

problems of communication when, years later, after returning to America in 1815, he produced the famous code system which was named after him.

Another visitor to London as a young man was **Tom Moore** (1779–1852) the Irish poet, who, in 1799, at the age of 20, came here to study law. He lodged at **85 George Street, W1**, which he remembers in his memoirs: 'I paid six shillings per week. The neighbourhood was the chief residence of those poor French emigrants who were then swarming into London, and in the back room of my floor was an old curé, the head of whose bed was placed tête-à-tête with mine, so that (the partition being very thin) not a snore escaped me . . . A poor émigré bishop, occupies the floor below me, and, as he had many callers, and no servants, his resource, in order to save trouble, was having a square board hung up in the hall, on one side of which was written "The Bishop's at Home" and on the other "The Bishop's gone out" so that callers had but to look up at this placard to know their fate.'

Moore, handsome, witty, and cheekily opportunistic, quickly established himself in London society. He became very fashionable, and for some time no soirée was complete without Tom Moore singing his pertinent ballads, accompanying himself on the piano. The wealthy fawned over him, and he basked in their adulation. On one occasion, however, in 1806, he was too clever by half. A book of his verse had been critically savaged in the *Edinburgh Review* by Jeffrey. This alone was enough to cross him. But when reports of personal slights against him from the same source reached his ears, Moore issued a challenge to a duel. Jeffrey had said something about Moore's 'deliberate design to corrupt the minds of innocent maidens with his wanton fancies'. 'To this', wrote Moore, 'I beg leave to answer you are a liar, yes, sir, a liar, and I choose to adopt this harsh and vulgar mode of defiance

in order to prevent at once all equivocation between us.' The dual was to take place on Chalk Farm Fields. It now occurred to Moore that he had no pistols. He had once, in handling a weapon of this sort, blown his thumb off 'and that was the whole, I believe, of my previous acquaintance with firearms'. Eventually two were obtained, and early one morning a few days later, Moore and Jeffrey met for the first time. 'Beautiful morning' said Jeffrey while the seconds withdrew behind some trees for the purpose of loading the pistols. Eventually the weapons were handed to the principals, the seconds 'retired to a little distance, the pistols on both sides raised, and we waited for the signal to fire, when some police officers, whose approach none of us had noticed, and who were within a second of being too late, rushed out from a hedge behind Jeffrey, and one of them struck at Jeffrey's pistol with his staff, knocked it to some distance into the field, while another running over to me, took possession of mine. We were then replaced in our respective carriages and conveyed crestfallen to Bow Street'. Moore, in fact, was speedily released, along with Jeffrey, and was on the verge of making a big splash about his heroics in the newspapers when it was discovered that Jeffrey's gun had no bullet in it! The significance of this was open to all sorts of interpretations – especially since Moore had provided the guns and arranged the seconds. So, instead of the story that Moore longed to print, he 'found himself held up to the public as an ass in a lion's skin, a hero who had only courage enough to stand before a leadless pistol'. Byron wrote in *English Bards and Scotch Reviewers*:

'Can none remember that eventful day,
That ever glorious, almost fatal fray,
When Little's* leadless pistols met his eye,
And Bow Street myrmidions stood laughing by?'

* A few of Moore's early pieces were published under the pen name of 'Thomas Little'.

Moore of course sent his own version to the newspapers, pointing out, correctly, that the bullet from Jeffrey's gun had, unnoticed, fallen into the grass during the loading, but no editor was going to spoil his circulation with such a racy alternative story to print.

Edward Gibbon (1737–1792), who is commemorated at **7 Bentinck Street, W1** was a much more genteel person altogether. He lived his heroics in his mighty *History of the Roman Empire*, much of which was written here in this house. His father had left him a goodly sum of money, and much of it had been spent on this house, which he called 'the best house in the world'. Certainly he was well looked after. His staff consisted of a housekeeper, butler, cook, and four maids. Not bad for a bachelor of 35! The rooms were hung with blue flock-wallpaper, and the decorations were by Adam. A glimpse of his life here comes from a letter to a friend written in September, 1774. 'Yesterday morning, about half an hour after seven, as I was destroying an army of barbarians, I heard a double rap at the door, and my friend . . . was soon introduced. After some idle conversation he told me that if I was desirous of becoming a member of parliament, he had an independent seat very much at my service. This is a fine opening for me, and if next spring I should take my seat and publish my book, it will be a very memorable era in my life.' The book was an enormous success when it was published, so much so that Gibbon wrote 'the first edition was exhausted in a few days . . . my book was on every table . . . almost on every toilette . . .'

Thomas Young (1773–1829) man of science is commemorated at **48 Welbeck Street, W1** where he lived from 1802–1825; **John Loughborough Pearson** (1817–1897) the architect, at **13 Mansfield Street, W1**, the house later lived in by another architect, **Sir Edwin Lutyens. John Flaxman**, the famous sculptor, lived at **7 Greenwell Street, W1**, and **George Richmond**, the painter at **20 York Street,** **W1, Edmond Malone** (1741–1812) the Shakespearian scholar lived at **40 Langham Street, W1** and **Elizabeth Garrett Anderson**, the first woman to qualify as a doctor in Britain is commemorated at **20 Upper Berkeley Street, W1**. Finally, amongst these brief mentions, **William Strang**, the painter and etcher, lived at **20 Hamilton Terrace, W1**.

The birthplace of **Dante Gabriel Rossetti** is commemorated at **110 Hallam Street, W1**, (see Rossetti also page 21). His father was an Italian poet and revolutionary in exile. At the time of Dante's birth, he was earning a slender income teaching Italian. Later he was to become Professor of Italian at the King's College, in the Strand. Rossetti's brother wrote that 'the household was of narrow means . . . I suppose the years were few in which Rossetti (senior) made more than an annual £300, and it must generally have been less'. The family existed, therefore 'on a careful, but not stingy economy'. The house itself was 'a fairly neat but decidedly small one. It was smaller inside than views from the outside would suggest'. In fact it was so small inside that it lacked not only a nursery but also a study, and when the father came home 'in the dusk, fagged with his round of teaching . . . after dining he would lie down flat on the hearth rug close by the fire, and fall asleep for an hour or two, snoring vigorously. Beside him would stand our old familiar tabby cat, poised on her haunches, and holding on by the foreclaws inserted into the fender bars, warming her furry front.' Rossetti was a kind father and would often allow 'his four children to litter and rollick about the room while he plodded through some laborious matter of literary composition'. There was 'besides cards, a rocking horse, a spinning top, a tee-to-tum, ball, nine pins, blindman's buff, and puss-in-the-corner to amuse us all hardly anything else in the way of games . . . even marbles we never rightly learned, not efficient kite flying, still less anything to be called athletics . . .' Not that the children seemed to mind very much.

Left: *The statue of Dante Gabriel Rossetti reposes restfully in front of his old home in Cheyne Walk. The well-ordered existence of life as a child in Hallam Street was far removed from the eccentricity of Rossetti's habits and pleasures in later years.*
Below: *This alleyway behind Stothard's residence in Newman Street nostalgically captures a little old world charm not often found any longer in Central London.*

They were well, and lovingly looked after by their mother 'an assiduous housewife from day to day and from year to year ... infallibly upright, with no indebtedness'.

His mother was Dante's first teacher. A warm, cultured woman, who loved to welcome other Italians to the house to hear the latest news from her homeland, she proved remarkably good at instructing her young son. By the age of five he could read and write, and was soon speaking fluent Italiana too. Dante's first poem, called *The Slaves*, was written at the age of six, and filled nine small pages in his large handwriting. The subject of his first painting, recalls his brother in his memoirs about Rossetti, was his rocking horse. 'At the age of about four he stationed himself in the passage leading to the street door, and with a pencil of our father's began drawing his rocking horse ... A milkman came in at the moment, and was not a little surprised. "I saw a baby making a picture", he said to the servant. Having once begun, Dante never stopped. He produced other infantile drawings some in pen and ink, many of them coloured ... two represent his dormouse 'Dwanging', and as 'Dwanging' hardly existed at a date later than the completion of Dante's sixth birthday, 12 May 1834, these must have been extremely early affairs.'

Two years later the family moved to 56 Charlotte Street, W1.

Thomas Stothard (1755–1834) the painter and illustrator, is commemorated at **28 Newman Street, W1**. In his lifetime he completed over 5000 book illustrations, and probably nearer to double that number. His illustrations for books included those for *Rape of The Lock*, *Childe Harold*, Walton's *The Compleat Angler* and the *De Cameron*. His time in this house was attended by endless troubles, and is vividly portrayed by his daughter in law, Mrs Bray in her *Life of Thomas Stothard*. He had begun exhibiting at the Academy when he was only

This London County Council plaque to Thomas Stothard, the painter and illustrator, erected in 1911, is unique in that it has been specially shaped to fit the building. Some 23 of this type of plaque were erected between 1907 and 1921, and were made in stone, lead or bronze.

20. At dinner one night to some fellow Academicians, the family plate was used. The next morning this valuable silver had completely disappeared. The matter was very puzzling for, as far as Stothard could see, the doors and windows seemed untouched. The robbery, therefore, was unaccountable. Many years later a criminal in Newgate confessed to how the crime was committed. The cook had agreed to leave the drawing room windows unbarred on the night of the party. The plate was carried off in a sack and consigned to the melting pot before the next morning.

While the loss of the silver was saddening, it in no way equalled the tragedy befalling Stothard's eldest son, who was accidentally shot and killed by a schoolfellow. Three months before his death, Stothard and his wife were disturbed one night by loud, violent shrieks coming from the boy's bedroom. 'He slept in an attic of the house in Newman Street', Mrs Bray tells us, 'as soon as he could speak to them, with a mingled expression of tears and awe, said that he had seen a vision full of terror in his sleep. A man, habited as a watchman had appeared to him holding in his hand a white flag, on the corner of which was a small spot of blood. The man then waved the flag over his head, until . . . the small spot spread itself out, and so increased that the whole of the white flag at length became covered with blood. This dream made the deepest impression on the boy. He, in some measure, recorded it the next day, writing, with his own hand, in red chalk, on the white washed wall, by the side of his bed: "And your young men shall see visions, and your old men shall dream dreams'. From that day the little room where he slept was called The Dreaming Room, and so long as Stothard lived the writing on the wall was never suffered to be effaced.' That such a vision should appear to the boy just three months before his death was strange enough. The experience of his mother and father on the very day of his death, however, was stranger still. They were inside the house, preparing to go out for a walk. The mother was standing with Stothard, and suddenly looked past him, thinking she had seen the son. She exclaimed 'Tom, what do you want here? But, as you are here, go down and tell the servant to bring up my gown'. Stothard, knowing that he had just given money to his son to go out, and that the boy had gone a half an hour before, was naturally astonished, and asked his wife what she meant since the boy was not there. 'I saw him this instant standing by the bed' was her reply, and she added that, when she spoke, the boy seemed to stoop down and vanish. Almost immediately afterwards there was a knock at the door and two strangers were admitted . . . their errand was to tell the death of the much loved son. Interestingly, the source of this account on the occasion of Stothard's son's death is not Mrs Bray, but Stothard's biographer, Coxhead. That two writers have recorded separately such strange tales about the Stothard household does lend an air of intriguing mystery to this house.

Mystery is also recalled by the house at **65 Gloucester Place, W1**, where **Wilkie Collins** (1824–1889) the novelist, lived. Wilkie Collins, friend and collaborator with Charles Dickens, and author of the celebrated *Woman in White* (1860) and *The Moonstone* (1868) was effectively the first ever English crime writer of what has now become a superbly rich literary genre.

BLOOMSBURY

Although Bloomsbury, lying to the south of Euston Road and north of Oxford Street, is the home of the British Museum, London University, teaching and specialist hospitals, publishers, academic and professional bodies, the special intellectual flavour of the area was greatly contributed by the famous Bloomsbury Group. Three plaques in London mark the development of this literary and artistic group. Since its story is a distinct one, and therefore can be told chronologically, it is necessary to start not in Bloomsbury at all, but in Kensington, at **22 Hyde Park Gate, SW7,** where **Leslie Stephen** is commemorated and where his daughter, Virginia Woolf, spent the first 22 years of her life. (See also page 39).

Leslie Stephen (1832–1904) scholar and writer, lived in this house from 1876 until his death in 1904. He had moved here following the death of his first wife, the younger of Thackeray's two daughters. Stephen, some years before, had been bound for an academic career at Cambridge where he was taking holy orders. Quite suddenly, he became an agnostic, declined to take part any more in the religious life of his college, so was asked to forfeit his position there by the Master lest his lack of faith in the established order of things should influence anybody else. Stephen left Cambridge for London to make some sort of a career for himself in literature.

At Cambridge he had been a fine athlete. He was also an accomplished climber, and it was through his mountaineering ability, and his love of Switzerland in particular, that he came to be appointed as editor of *The Alpine Journal.* The appointment was a successful one, and in 1871 he became editor of the *Cornhill Magazine,* an assignment he was to hold for 11 years. Now married for a second time, it was here that his wife, Julia, started their family. Their third child, Virginia, was born in this house on January 25 1882.

Quentin Bell writes in his biography of his aunt, Virginia Woolf, that the house in Hyde Park Gate was tall, and dark, with a medium sized back garden. The children's nurseries were at the top of the house. Since by the following year there was now a fourth child, Leslie Stephen's rather gloomy study downstairs, where he displayed certain relics from his mountaineering days must have fairly shuddered from the din up above. 'Miss Virginia', Stephen wrote in a letter to a friend, referring to some of these family quarrels, 'aged two and a half, scratches her brother, aged four. I insist upon and ultimately obtain an apology or a kiss. She looks very thoughtful for some time then says, Papa, why have we got nails?' The noise of the children must have sometimes driven Leslie Stephen away from the house altogether. Luckily for him, he greatly enjoyed walking. Once, much younger, he had walked home to London all the way from Cambridge, and even now he still enjoyed an extended 'potter', sometimes as much as thirty miles in a day. On Sundays he would occasionally join 'The Tramps', a small group of Sunday walkers he had formed amongst his literary friends. Charles Darwin, living at Down in Kent, Tyndall at Hindhead and George Meredith at Box Hill, were all visited by 'The Tramps' with Stephen at their head.

In 1881, Stephen was appointed editor of the new *Dictionary of National Biography.* It was an enormous task, and one which was eventually to wear him out, but not before he had successfully established that the Dictionary should be a work of major historical biography.

Another literary landmark within the family took place at this time, Virginia's debut as a storyteller. Bell tells us, 'When the lights had been extinguished, all save that which came from the dying coal fire, she would begin her tale'. The stories involved the discovery of gold beneath the nursery floor, 'and this treasure trove would purchase enormous meals of bacon and eggs, the favourite diet of the young at 22 Hyde Park Gate'.

Leslie and Julia Stephen had already decided to educate their children themselves, and though tempers were frequently lost by both parents, as their small children failed to decline properly in Greek, or add up simple sums on their fingers, the days seemed to pass without any major traumas. Outside school hours there were walks in Kensington Gardens, and enthralling Alpine stories from Leslie. In addition, Virginia was allowed increasing freedom in her father's library. Summer holidays in Cornwall, the publication in London of Virginia's family newspaper *The Hyde Park Gate News*, when the young editor/journalist was only nine, and the evident success of the *Dictionary of National Biography* all should have been important strands in a growing sense of unity and security within the walls of 22 Hyde Park Gate. In fact the very reverse was true. 'Hyde Park Gate' wrote Michael Holroyd in a *Times* book review of *Virginia Woolf* by Quentin Bell: 'came to represent the threat of death, madness and disaster, for Virginia's upbringing, though outwardly secure, was interspersed by a series of traumatic shocks.'

Predictably, perhaps, Leslie Stephen was no longer a well man. He had collapsed first in 1888, followed by two more attacks very shortly. In addition he suffered from insomnia, and a completely unwarranted neurosis over his financial security. On one occasion he told Edmund Gosse in great shame and secrecy that he was ruined, that there was only £1000 left. 'Gosse and other men of letters', Bell writes, 'decided that something must be done; but first it was necessary to know more about the financial situation of the Stephen family.' But a tactful enquiry at Leslie Stephen's bank revealed that he was not ruined at all. The balance of his drawing account had slid a little to £1000, while his income and his capital remained totally unchanged! Julia, who by now had persuaded him to withdraw from his labours with the Dictionary, was far from well herself as she struggled to look after him, but the calm needed for his recovery was frequently battered by horrifying outbursts from Virginia's half sister, Laura, who was showing increasing signs of severe mental instability which produced terrible stresses within the household. And if all this tension was not enough, Virginia, unbeknown to her parents, was also having to cope with the horrible advances made to her by her half brother, George Duckworth. 'I still shiver with shame', she wrote many years afterwards, 'at the memory of my half brother, standing me on a ledge, aged about six or so, exploring my private parts.' Quite suddenly in 1895, her mother, worn out and harrassed by her work of looking after Leslie, caught influenza and died. 'Her death', said Virginia, 'was the greatest disaster that could happen.' For George Duckworth, Julia's death was just another excuse to throw himself upon Virginia's bed, kissing and embracing her, pretending to administer comfort at her bereavement. After Julia's death, what happiness there was in the household was induced by Stella, another half sister, who made herself indispensable to all by spearheading some form of family unity once more. Leslie, in particular, relied on her tremendously. But when she too suddenly died in 1897, the house was utterly bleak. Leslie came to rely increasingly on Virginia, a heavy burden for so young, sensitive and shaken a girl. Michael Holroyd writes that Leslie, though lovable to his friends, was 'ruthless with his family, inflicting on them a savage emotional blackmail'. Virginia had already

suffered the first of the nervous breakdowns that were to punctuate the rest of her life. It is doubtful if she could have endured things for very much longer as they were. Her relief, therefore, can be understood when Leslie Stephen died of cancer in 1904, and the family had the opportunity to move away from the house in Hyde Park Gate.

'By the time the world had heard of Bloomsbury' wrote Desmond MacCarthy, himself a member of the inner circle, 'Bloomsbury as a group had ceased to exist'. The point about Bloomsbury was that it was different. The house at 46 Gordon Square, WC1, to which Virginia and her sister Vanessa had moved in the autumn of 1904 was spacious and well lit, quite different from the interior of their father's old home. It was also a long distance away. Though the move shocked their relatives 'it was', Bell writes, 'precisely the virtue of the place that it lay so far from that dark house of many tragedies in which they had grown up'. The difference, too, about Bloomsbury was in meeting a generation of people and ideas completely different from those who had seemed enshrined in the very fittings and furniture of the house at Hyde Park Gate. Virginia was 22, her elder brother, Thoby, who was now reading law after finishing at Cambridge some time before, was 24. It was through him that a brilliant circle of people began meeting in Bloomsbury. Lytton Strachey, Duncan Grant, Maynard Keynes, Roger Fry, Desmond MacCarthy, and Leonard Woolf and Clive Bell, Quentin's father, shortly to marry Vanessa Stephen, all congregated here. **Lytton Strachey** himself was to settle in **Gordon Square, WC1,** at **No. 51,** where he is commemorated today by a Blue Plaque. 'Bloomsbury' recalls Quentin Bell in a press interview, 'on the whole didn't go in for being brilliant in the way of Wilde of Beerbohm, but it was candid and vivacious.' Virginia had started to write serious criticism for the *Times*

Literary Supplement, and to teach at Morley College. Her health seemed to be recovering. This seemed to be a period of stabilisation. Then in 1906 came another disaster when, after contacting a mysterious illness on a trip to Greece, Thoby died suddenly. This catastrophe abruptly ended the short period of happiness Virginia had found. It meant, too, that she would have to move from Gordon Square because Vanessa, two days after Thoby's death 'had turned to Clive Bell for comfort and agreed to marry him'.

The commemorative plaque to **Virginia Woolf** (1882–1941) is at **29 Fitzroy Square, W1,** a pleasant house which had once been Bernard Shaw's old home. Here, in 1907, she moved in with Adrian, her surviving brother. She was to live here for four years until moving to 38 Brunswick Square, WC1 in 1911, the year before she agreed to marry Leonard Woolf.

Virginia Woolf's drawing room at Fitzroy Square was central to her life here. The Thursday evening gatherings, started by Thoby in Gordon Square, were re-instituted, and to them came a dazzling succession of literary and artistic figures. Apart from the guests, the drawing room was inhabited by her dog Hans which, recalls Bell, 'delighted in extinguishing visitors' matches with its paws', as well as, on one occasion, when Virginia was giving Lady Strachey tea, performing upon the hearthrug in a manner which ought to have been kept for the street, an action, which, adds Bell 'both guest and hostess thought it best to disregard'! For Virginia Woolf, these years at Fitzroy Square were a period of consolidation. The doctors, once more, were satisfied with her health.

As for her writing, she was steadily adding to her literary poise, priming herself for the moment when she could assume her natural place in the front ranks of English novelists. Her struggles were not so much with her talents, and what to do with them, as with her existence, and where it was taking her. Perhaps inevitably, therefore, she made light of her helpless drift, concealing these grim forebodings behind a veil of absurd clowning which amused so many of her friends. She was known for her gaiety, her jokes, her delight in gentle outrage and her fun. And while her life was to end in melancholy fashion some thirty years later, this house in Fitzroy Square has many smiling memories of her, and none more happy than that of a brisk February morning in 1910 when Virginia, with five companions, drove to Paddington Station and took a train to Weymouth. 'She wore', wrote Bell, 'a turban, a fine gold chain hanging to her waist and an embroidered caftan. Her face was black. She sported a very handsome moustache and beard.' Three others in the party were similarly dressed, while the other two wore bowler hats, one of them being 'convincingly attired as an official of the Foreign Office'. As soon as Virginia and her five men friends settled giggling in the luxury of their first class railway compartment, they effectively became the Emperor of Abyssinia and his entourage, on their way to inspect the flagship of The Commander-In-Chief Home Fleet, the mighty H.M.S. *Dreadnought*, then anchored in Weymouth Bay, to which a telegram, 'purporting to come from the Foreign Office' had been sent announcing the Emperor's impending arrival. 'The "Dreadnought Hoax" – to give it the name by which it became famous – was, essentially, to be a repetition of the Zanzibar escapade', says Bell. He was referring to an earlier practical joke carried out by one of the party while still an undergraduate, when, posing as the Sultan of Zanzibar, he had successfully hoodwinked the Mayor of Cambridge and his top officials for a whole day while on an official visit to the University. Virginia, says Bell, was delighted to be asked to take part in this later hoax, and, by all accounts, played her part magnificently. The party was received at

Weymouth Station by a flag lieutenant who 'saluted the Emperor with becoming gravity ... there was a barrier to restrain the crowd and the Imperial party proceeded with dignity to where a little steam launch lay in readiness to carry it out to the fleet anchored in the bay'. The inspection of the Guard of Honour, and the rest of the visit on board Britain's most modern, and most secret battleship, went off impeccably. The Imperial party were shown anything they cared to be curious about, much to the red-faced indignation of the First Lord of the Admiralty who had to answer several questions in the House of Lords some days later after the story of the escapade had been slipped to the press. For a few days Virginia and her friends were headline news. It was a rare interlude of harmless excess in a life fated by catastrophe, and from which Virginia Woolf herself, in the end, could not escape. She died in 1941. This plaque was erected in 1975.

'Bloomsbury' wrote Desmond MacCarthy in 1933, by way of an epilogue to the times he had enjoyed in its various houses, 'is neither a movement, nor a push, but only a group of old friends; whose affection and respect for each other has stood the test of nearly thirty years and whose intellectual candour makes their company agreeable to each other.' It was never a movement: '... and so far from being a mutual admiration society, "Bloomsbury" is the last place where a Bloomsburian, who has just written a book, would look for that enthusiastic amazement at his achievement which authors enjoy most.'

This pleasing absence of self-reverence, one might almost say self-importance, was certainly not the case in the middle of the previous century at **17 Red Lion Square, WC1**, where a plaque commemorates the stay there of **Dante Gabriel Rossetti** (see pages 21, 85, 86), **William Morris** (1834–1896) and **Edward Burne-Jones** (1833–1898). Artistic purism and its attainment was everything to these high priests of the pre-

Raphaelite movement. Even so, despite some of the faintly pompous ideals of this group, life for its foundling fathers was not without its human side. Burne-Jones, a native of Birmingham, had intended to take holy orders at the time he met Rossetti and came under his influence. He abandoned his theological studies at Oxford, and came to live with Rossetti in London.

The landlord at Red Lion Square, realising Rossetti was of an artistic temperament, and that painting might well be one of his activities on the premises stipulated, Rossetti recalled some years later, 'that the models are to be kept under some gentlemanly restraint as some artists sacrifice the dignity of art to the baseness of passion'! Georgina Burne-Jones wrote of her brother in her memoirs: 'Morris and Edward had the first floor, on which there were three rooms; a large one in front with the middle window cut up to the ceiling for a painting light, a medium size room behind this, which Edward had, and a smaller one which was Morris's. Some French people named Fauconnier, who were feather dressers were the tenants of the house, and carried on their business below.' Burne-Jones himself wrote of the move: 'I think to see me in the midst of a removal is to behold the most abjectly pitiable sight in nature; books, boxes, boots, bedding, baskets, coats, pictures, armour, hats, easel – tumble and rumble and jumble. After all, one must confess there is an unideal side to a painter's life – a remark which has received weight in the fact that the exceedingly respectable housekeeper we got has just turned in upon us in the most unequivocal state of intoxication!' This was Red Lion Mary, who in time became an excellent needlewoman and who did anything for 'her boys', as she called them. Morris taught her to embroider most successfully. The firm of Morris & Co. was set up at 8 Red Lion Square. The place was a centre of industry, with Ruskin visiting

Bottom right: *The foreground poster declaring a public meeting to prevent a return to the 30s in this photograph of Lord Eldon's house in Bedford Square, WC1 is politically well in context for a residence that was stormed in 1815 by the poor and unemployed.*
Top right: *A marble bust of Spencer Perceval by Joseph Nollekens. The bust, which was executed a year after Perceval's assassination, in 1813, can be seen in the Wellington Museum, Apsley House, Hyde Park Corner.*
Left: *John Harrison's plaque at 119 High Holborn, WC1.*

them at work often to pass comments on their various creations. But they took their recreations too. Once on a rowing trip on the Thames the group of them had ventured too far and too late, being forced to spend some of their short supply of money in getting home. 'At last we reached Red Lion Square and were very late in coming back', wrote George Birkbeck, a friend. 'At night five mattresses were spread over the carpetless floor, and there I slept amidst painters and poets. Next morning I watched Burne-Jones painting some lilies in the gardens of the square. It was, I believe, the first time he painted in oils.' In 1858, William Morris became engaged to a Miss Burden, and Burne-Jones realised he would have to find somewhere else to live. Georgina Burne-Jones wrote that 'The Red Lion Rooms were transferred to a Mr Swan ... and Mary stayed on as a housekeeper to him, still working on pieces of embroidery for Morris until her own marriage a short while later.' The plaque was erected in 1922.

HOLBORN

Holborn is the smallest of the old London Metropolitan boroughs, covering no more than 405 acres. It is also one of the least residential areas of inner London, comprising of much commercial territory. Few plaques, therefore, are to be found here. At **59–60 Lincoln's Inn Fields, WC2** there is one to **Spencer Perceval (1762–1812)**, the Prime Minister, who was assassinated in 1812, and a second Prime Minister, **Lord Eldon (1751–1838)** is commemorated at **6 Bedford Square, WC1.** Eldon had to protect his family and possessions at this house one night in 1815 when the London mob, protesting against the Corn Laws, attacked the homes of many well known politicians. Eldon was a strong man, with a fierce tongue too. Troops guarding other establishments not far away, including the British Museum, were called, and Eldon, a determined advocate of hanging, even for the most menial of offences, left the rioters in no doubt what their fate would be if they tampered any more with his property.

FURTHER NAMES COMMEMORATED IN HOLBORN

John Howard (1726–1790) the great prison reformer, is commemorated at **23 Great Ormond Street, WC1; Thomas Earnshaw,** watchmaker, on the site of **119 High Holborn, WC1,** and **John Harrison** (1693–1776) inventor of the marine chronometer, on the site of **Summit House,** in Red Lion Square. **William Lethaby** (1857–1931) architect, is commemorated on the walls of the **Central School of Arts, Southampton Row, WC1,** of which he was first Principal, and **Dr Robert Willan** (1757–1812) is remembered at **10 Bloomsbury Square, WC1,** for his advances in the field of dermatology.

PADDINGTON

At **35 Gloucester Square, W2,** lived **Robert Stephenson,** (1803–1859) the engineer. He moved here in 1847, and was by then engaged on, or had completed, most of his major works. His projects included the building of the railway from Alexandria to Cairo; the erection of the Conway Bridge; the great border viaduct over the Tweed; the Great Victoria Bridge of the St Lawrence at Montreal, and now, during the time he was living in this house, the task of linking Christiania and the Miösen Lake in Norway. The sheer scope of his commitments led, inevitably, to an extremely busy life, which, while he was in London, centred on the house at Gloucester Square, where he also had an office. Jefferson, in his *Life of Robert Stephenson* recalls the hectic atmosphere in the house when writing about a visitor who called to discuss urgent business with Stephenson, and 'found every reception room occupied by a crowd of persons'. Being much engaged, and wishing to employ his time with correspondence until he could have an interview with Robert Stephenson, he asked the servant to show him into a room where he could be by himself and write his letters in quiet. 'If you want, that, Sir', the man answered, 'you must go upstairs into one of the bedrooms, for every sitting room is occupied with gentlemen insisting on seeing Mr Stephenson, although they know he is unwell.' Stephenson's ill health under such pressure of work was inevitable. Even on Sundays he rarely relaxed, although the large luncheon parties he threw, were, by all accounts, pleasant occasions. The guests included many chiefs of literature and science, and 'the drawing room that was so liberally stocked with works of curious contrivance

Lord Randolph Churchill as seen by Spy in 'Vanity Fair', 1880, when the politician was in his thirty-second year.

and philosophical toys that they had almost the appearance of a museum' resounded to the conversation of the guests until nearly supper time. Stephen's only shield in this exhausting and ceaseless round was his brother-in-law, who, apart from being one of his closest personal friends, also lived in at Gloucester Square, and administered much of Stephenson's business. His death suddenly in 1853 left Stephenson grief-stricken, distraught, and utterly lonely. He spent twelve months in Thomas's Hotel, Berkeley Square, before he could bring himself to return to the empty house in Paddington. Stephenson died here in 1859, after catching a severe chill in Norway attending a function in his honour to the completion of the Christiania-Miösen engineering link.

Marie Taglioni (1809–1884) the ballet dancer, who in the mid-nineteenth century had been such a favourite with all the Royal families of Europe, returned to London for one year in 1875 when she was nearly seventy, and lived at **14 Connaught Square, W2**. Taglioni, a trim little figure in black, lived here to instruct the children of nobility in deportment and dancing.

In 1874 Winston Churchill, future Prime Minister, had been born at Blenheim Palace, Woodstock. Lady Randolph Churchill, his mother, was a refreshingly independent woman in London society. It was characteristic of her, therefore to choose, when she was looking for a new London home some ten years later, to choose a house quite different from the usual Mayfair and Belgravia drab residences where so many of her friends, and her husband's parliamentary colleagues, lived. Writing in her *Reminiscences* she said: 'The year 1883 saw us in a new house in Connaught Place. "Tyburnia", our friends called it, as on the railings opposite our windows, which faced Hyde Park, there was a small tablet to mark the site of Tyburn Gate. Often I thought of the

Left: *A portrait of Lord Randolph Churchill.*
Below: *The portrait of J. M. Barrie by Nicholson which hangs in the Scottish National Portrait Gallery.*

thousands of poor wretches who had been hanged there, and sometimes wondered if the house would be full of wailing ghosts, but frankly, I never saw or heard one.' The house at **2 Connaught Place, W2**, commemorated as the residence of **Lord Randolph Churchill**, the statesman, was also one of the first houses in England to be lit by electricity. 'I remember', Lady Randolph continues, 'the fiasco of a dinner party we gave to show it (the electricity) off, when the lights went out in the middle of the feast, just as we were expatiating on its beauties, our guests having to remain in utter darkness until the lamps and candles, which had been relegated to the lower regions, were unearthed.' It was in these 'lower regions' that the dynamo was placed, being 'in the cellar underneath the street, so that the noise of it greatly excited all the horses as they approached our door'. The house, most daringly for the time, was painted throughout in white, and with delicate pieces of French and Italian furniture, and wall decorations from Japan and China, it was one of the most sophisticated salons in London. Winston himself knew little of the house, being away at school for much of the time his parents were there.

J. M. Barrie (1860–1937) novelist and playwright, is commemorated at **100 Bayswater Road, W2** where he and his wife lived briefly before moving to the country. It is a pleasant Regency house, with views across to Kensington Gardens, and it was here, in his large study, that Barrie wrote *Peter Pan*, which was first produced at Christmas 1904.

Guglielmo Marconi (1874–1937) the pioneer of wireless communication, lived at **71 Hereford Road, W2**, in 1896 for a few months. He had perfected his experiments in wireless transmissions in 1894, but the Italian Government had shown no interest in the project. Marconi packed his equipment into suitcases and travelled to Britain, settling in rooms at the top floor in Hereford Road. Undeterred by the breakages to several of his valuable pieces during his trip across Europe, Marconi used this room to prove to officials from the General Post Office how revolutionary his equipment was.

FURTHER NAMES COMMEMORATED IN PADDINGTON

John Claudius Loudon (1783–1843) the architectural writer, horticulturist and journalist is commemorated at **3 Porchester Terrace, W2**; **Alice Meynell** (1847–1922) the poet and essayist, is commemorated at **47 Palace Court, W2**; the little known **Olive Schreiner** (1855–1920) the authoress lived briefly at **16 Portsea Place, W2** in the 1880s before returning to South Africa. **Charles Manby**, civil engineer, is commemorated at **60 Westbourne Terrace, W2**, and **Alexander Herzen** the Russian political thinker, stayed briefly at **1 Orsett Terrace, Paddington, W2**. Finally, in Paddington, **Sir Rowland Hill** (1795–1879) founder of the national postal service, is remembered at **1 Orme Square, W2**.

NORTH & NORT

EAST LONDON

ISLINGTON

Joseph Chamberlain (1836–1914) the statesman is commemorated at **25 Highbury Place, N1.** He moved with his family here in 1845, after living nine years in Camberwell, where he had been born. Islington was to be Chamberlain's home for the next ten years until he went to Birmingham where the seeds of his great political career were laid. In Lewis's *History and Topography of St Mary Islington*, Highbury Place is described then as '. . . a fine row of houses embracing a beautiful view on both sides. It is remarkable for its healthy situation. It consists of 39 houses built on a large scale, but varying in size, all having good gardens . . . the road is private, and frequented only by the carriages passing to and from the several dwellings.' Chamberlain enjoyed a secure childhood here. His home life was happy, and his mother, a sweet and lovable woman 'exercised a powerful influence over her children'. They were taught to think, and to make independent decisions based on firm and unfussy religious principles. There could have been no better breeding ground for one of the very few British statesmen of the nineteenth century who achieved power on merit and not through influence or patronage. Joseph was sent as a day pupil to a nearby school, but showed such attainment that he soon knew more than those whose task it was to teach him. At that point it was suggested to his father that it was high time Joseph went on elsewhere. At the age of 14, Joseph entered University College School where he was to stay for two years, gaining great distinction in mathematics. In 1852, at the age of 16, he left school to enter his father's business, a cordwainers, beginning at the bottom and entering 'not the counting house, but the workshop, sitting side by side with the shoemakers'. But it was not long before Chamberlain needed the challenge of greater commercial stimulation than his father's small firm allowed. Two years later, aged 18, he and a cousin in Birmingham joined forces in the business of making wooden screws. That city, then, was one of the most formidable and rapidly expanding industrial centres of the world. Chamberlain and his cousin, by shrewd business acumen, and a willingness to enjoy hard work, quickly prospered. For 20 years Chamberlain continued at his work, establishing himself in the meantime as a powerful spokesman for Birmingham's needs in the national forum. It was no surprise when in 1873, aged only 37, he was made Lord Mayor of that important city, and, a year later, returned to Parliament where, in a long and impressive political career, he never deviated from the principles of honesty and integrity he had learned from his mother in his Islington home.

Charles Lamb is commemorated at **64 Duncan Terrace, N1**, which was occupied by this famous essayist and his sister, Mary, with whom he lived, from 1823 until 1827. Lamb was then 48, and on the point of retirement from The East India Company. This was the first house he had owned, and, from a letter to a friend in September 1823, his delight in his new home plainly shows. 'When you come Londonward', he wrote, 'you will find me no longer in Covent Garden. I have a cottage in Colebrook (properly Colnbrook) Row, Islington; a good cottage, for it is detached; a white house with six good rooms; the New River (rather elderly by this time) runs (if a modest walking pace can be so termed) close to the foot of the house, and behind is a spacious garden with vines (I assure you) pears, strawberries, parsnips, leeks, carrots, cabbages, to delight the heart of old Alcinous. You enter without passage into cheerful dining room, all studded over and rough with books; and above is a lightsome drawing room, three windows, full of choice prints. I feel like a great lord, never having had a house before.' Lamb's joy, however, with the place, was not simply the pride of ownership. There was also the question of his sister, Mary, who years before in 1796, in a fit of insanity, had suddenly killed his mother. Lamb had always been fond of Mary, and undertook to look after her. Although she was to remain vulnerable to periodic seizures, she repaid him with sympathy and affection. The seizures had been very few of late, and Lamb must have felt as though a great cloud was lifting before him. Thomas Hood, however, who visited the Lambs here, obviously did not share Charles's optimism. He wrote of the house as 'a cottage of ungentility, for it had neither double coach house, nor wings', before adding ominously, 'like its tenant it stood alone'. Charles, however, felt a great deal more secure than his guest had recognised, for, as Edmund Blunden has written of Lamb '. . . in the hope of a normal home life, as well as from pure benevolence, they [Charles and Mary] adopted a little girl called Emma Isola, whose grandfather taught Wordsworth Italian. . . . Their devotion to Emma was faultless, and Lamb took the greatest pains to make his knowledge of literature and his gifts as a writer serve her education and her young friendships.' Crabbe-Robinson was a visitor to Lamb's house, and of his study he made the comment: 'He has the finest collection of shabby books I ever saw. Such a number of first rate works of genius, but filthy copies, which a delicate man would really hesitate touching is, I think, nowhere to be found.'

Posterity, however, cares far more for the memory of Charles Lamb and the excellence of his writings than for the pettiness of Crabbe-Robinson's reminiscences. It was here, in this study, that Charles Lamb, who for some years had been writing single essays under the pseudonym Elia, 'a person of that name, an Italian, was a fellow clerk of mine at The South Sea House' gathered those contributions together under a single volume. It was here also that he wrote some of his best verse. After work, he loved to walk across the fields and watch the sunset from the summit of the Canonbury Tower, and sit with his pipe at the local hostelry, happy that some semblance of peace had visited such a troubled life. But his health was not good and in the winter of 1824–5, he suffered a severe illness, and so retired from his work at the East India Company. In April of that year he wrote to Wordsworth: 'Here I am after 33 years' slavery, sitting in my room at 11 o'clock this finest of all April mornings, a freed man, with £441 a year for the remainder of my life . . . I came home for ever on Tuesday of last week. The incomprehensibleness of my condition overwhelmed me. It was like passing from life into eternity. . . . Mary wakes every morning with an obscure feeling that some good has happened to us.' Hazlitt wrote of Lamb in his retirement: 'He took much interest in the antiquities of "Merrie Islington". Queen Elizabeth's Walk became his favourite promenade in summer time, for its historical associations, its seclusion and its shade. He would sit silently contemplating the spangled heavens until the cold night air warned him to retire . . .'

In the daytime of that summer the garden afforded Lamb much pleasure, as he himself testifies. 'I am so taken up with pruning and gardening, quite a new sort of occupation for me. I have gathered my jarjonels, but my Windsor pears are backwards. The former were of exquisite raciness. . . .' There were other outdoor diversions, too. On one occasion a visitor, George Dyer, walked blindly into the New River (now underground at this site) that ran close to the foot of the house. 'George Dyer', writes Lamb, 'instead of keeping the slip that leads to the gate, had, deliberately, staff in hand, in broad open daylight, marched into the New River.... Who helped him out they can hardly tell ... but between 'em they got him drenched thro' and thro' ... a mob collected by that time and accompanied him in. "Send for the Doctor" they said; and a one-eyed fellow, dirty and drunk, was fetched from the public house at the end where it seems he lurks for the sake of picking up water practice, having formerly had a medal from The Humane Society for some rescue.'

While Lamb had been working in the City, he had always commuted there on foot. He only went to London occasionally now, sometimes to see his publishers, and once or twice to take Mary out shopping. But his health was deteriorating again, and he felt it wise to move. In 1827, the Lambs moved to Enfield, and then in 1833 to Edmonton where Charles died the following year.

One other pleasure that Charles and Mary Lamb took before moving away from Islington was the occasional visit to Sadlers Wells Theatre, then known at the Aquatic Theatre on account of the large number of water spectacles that were incorporated into the productions. These were soon to stop, however, when **Samuel Phelps**, the tragedian, commemorated at **8 Canonbury Square, N1,** took over the managership of the theatre. He wrote: 'I took over an obscure theatre in the North of London, and nearly the whole of my brethren in the profession, and many out of it, said it could not last a fortnight. It lasted eighteen years, and my stock in trade chiefly consisted of the plays of Shakespeare!' Phelps was determined to succeed at the theatre. But his friends were right in one respect, he had a very difficult task ahead of him. Coleman, in his *Memoirs of Samuel Phelps*, tells the whole story of what confronted Phelps on the opening night, when the production was Macbeth. It was performed, writes Coleman, amidst a '... hideous medley of fights, foul language, cat-

calls, shrieks, yells, oaths, blasphemy, obscenity, apples, oranges, nuts, biscuits, ginger beer, porter and pipes – pipes of all sorts and sizes were at work in the gallery, and pipes of all descriptions were at full blast in the pit ... cans of beer, each with a pint to drink from, were carried through the dense crowd at all stages of the tragedy ... sickly children in arms were squeezed out of shape in all parts of the house ... Fish was fried at the entrance doors, barricades of oyster shells emcumbered the pavements, expectant half price visitors to the gallery hurled defiant impertinence up the stairs, and danced a sort of carmagnole all round the building....' This sort of bedlam was enough to dampen any actor's heart, but Phelps was determined to succeed. Not only did the performance carry on and end 'his voice that was resonant on every word' carrying throughout the theatre, but in time, and a comparatively short time at that, the Islington mob had been silenced, and he was still playing to full houses of former rowdies who now went to the theatre to watch and listen to some of the greatest acting then on view throughout the country. Phelps was a great walker, and kept himself very fit. On the days when he was performing, his routine at home was a rigid one. He always took a sleep on the couch in his living room in Canonbury Square, waking at five o'clock in the afternoon when he drank two cups of tea and smoked a favourite cigar. Then, he and his wife, who had always dressed him, walked down to the theatre and he began preparing for the evening performance. Phelps's time at Islington was a triumph. He was admired and loved by the local theatregoers, and his resignation came as a sad shock to them. It happened when he discovered, to his great grief, that his wife had cancer. The news that the person on whom he relied most had a fatal condition threw him into a state of nervous breakdown. He could not go on stage after being dressed by her for so

Left: *A postcard printed in 1904 which shows the auditorium of the Collins Music Hall, at Islington Green, and on the right, Sam Collins, the chimney sweep, turned singer, after whom the famous Islington Music Hall was named.*
Below: *The exterior of Collins Music Hall, Islington Green, as it was in 1926, after being rebuilt from its original façade in 1895.*

Below: *George Leybourne, the great comedian, otherwise known as Champagne Charlie represented here in the middle of one of his comic song routines.*
Right: *The waspish face of Little Tich beams out from this sheet music cover. Harry Relph's six fingers – the result of in-breeding within his family – are plainly seen on his right hand.*

many years, and, rather than go through the heartbreaking search for somebody else as sympathetic as she was to all the strains and stresses that afflicted him both before, during and after his performances, he decided the end of his time at Sadlers Wells had come. He took his bow in front of his adoring audience at a series of special performances, and then retired to semi-obscurity in the house in Canonbury Square, continuing to live there after his wife's eventual death. He himself died in 1878, 16 years later.

While Phelps was encouraging and nurturing a new generation of theatregoers at Sadlers Wells, **Sam Collins** was doing the same for variety at the Landsdowne Arms on nearby Islington Green. Within a short space of time, this had become known as **Collins Music Hall**, and is one of the very few buildings in London to be commemorated by a plaque. It stands at **10–11 Islington Green, N1.** Collins, a chimney sweep turned artist, who specialised in Irish songs, had taken over the Landsdowne Arms in 1862. Old sketches show a typical London public house facing the roadway. Inside, one passed through a series of bars, then a large vestibule, before moving into the auditorium. The only advertisement in the street outside were three large, lovely, painted London lamposts. It was their familiar glare and the noise of cheerful laughter within that drew the 'greats' of Victorian and Edwardian Music Hall to play in the large auditorium. Before the theatre finally closed in 1858, Little Tich, Marie Lloyd, Charlie Chaplin, Vesta Tilley, Champagne Charlie, Dan Leno and Albert Chevalier and a host of other stars, had all stood on the boards here before the crowded Islington audience. Several of the artists themselves are commemorated by Blue Plaques. **Little Tich** (**Harry Relph** – 1868–1928), who is remembered at **93 Shirehall Park, Hendon,** had all the appearance of a slightly maniac dwarf. He was only four feet tall, and was born with an extra finger on each

BIG BOOT DANCE

AS PERFORMED WITH IMMENSE SUCCESS

BY LITTLE TICH.

Yours Truly "Little Tich"

Composed by
JOSEPH FREDERICKS

Copyright

LONDON

PRICE 4

FULL ORCHESTRA

SEPTETT

Below: *Albert Chevalier.*

hand. Paul Nash, the artist, has left us this impression of Little Tich at work: 'He was able to be funny in so many ways – in appearance . . . a face like Punch's but more intelligent, agile as a mongoose, but capable of the most absurd and alarming tumbles and gestures, and often a voice of many modulations from shrill girlish piping to gutteral innuendoes and sibilant "double entendres". But his strangest, most compelling assets were his feet. These were, I think, normal in themselves, but were habitually inserted into the most monstrous boots, long, narrow and flat, so long that he could bow from the boots, and lean over at almost an acute angle from the heels . . . his little stick held casually behind him begins to look like a little dog's tail and wag with pleasure. . . . The audience is not slow to get these signs and hoot and whistle rude whistles. . . .

If Little Tich offered his audience joyful vulgarity, and shared in it with them, Champagne Charlie (**George Leybourne**, commemorated at **136 Englefield Road, Islington, N1**) offered them vulgar sophistication, and pretended surprise when they found him so deliciously funny. Leybourne, who made his London debut in 1864, was a remarkably handsome man with a fine voice. Enormously popular with his audiences, he affected the luxury off stage that he pretended on it. He dressed in long coats with huge fur collars, and his ringed fingers were always ready with a poised cigar. His manager, not slow to capitalise on the chance of more publicity, insisted that Leybourne drove to and from engagements in a large carriage drawn by four white horses. Of course, Leybourne's fellow artists and competitors chanced some good humoured burlesque and mimicry, and at least one of them promptly started driving to and from his engagements in a farm cart drawn by four screeching donkeys!

Albert Chevalier (1861–1923) at **17 St Ann's Villas. W1**, was a successful 'coster' singer, who frequently entertained at smart West End mansions.

ST PANCRAS

About half a mile up the Hampstead Road from the Euston Road there stands, on the left-hand side, a tall, stuccoed house marked by a circular tablet. Here, at **263 Hampstead Road, NW1** lived **George Cruikshank**, the artist, from 1850 until his death in 1878. Cruikshank was 'a broad chested well built man, rather below the middle height, with a high forehead, blue grey eyes, a hook nose and a pair of fierce looking whiskers of a decidedly original pattern'. (Dictionary of National Biography). Cruikshank was nearing his sixtieth year when he moved here, and some of his best work was done in this house. Here, in 1853, he illustrated *Uncle Tom's Cabin* for John Cassell; here he did his 20 etchings for Robert Brough's *Life of Sir John Falstaff*, including the wonderful death of the knight; the delightful 'Epping Hunt' for Thomas Hood's *Whimsicalities* and the eight illustrations for *Peter Schlemihl*, which Thackeray thought so excellent.

The house, however, was more famous at the time not for the work he achieved in it, but because it was from here that Cruikshank conducted his campaign against drink. As a young man he had plenty of experience of the bottle. His father, Isaac Cruikshank, was a hopeless drunk, and had actually died as a result of winning a whisky drinking contest. Cruikshank had lurched the same way, too. Dickens had seen him walk into the library of his home in Devonshire Place after a night's celebrating, stinking of tobacco, beer and sawdust, afraid to go home. Another friend, W. H. Wills remembered Cruikshank being abandoned by his companions in the street one night as Cruikshank insisted on climbing a lamp post. But it had taken the death of a

friend to make Cruikshank realise how drink could destroy talent, and several of his drawings alluded to its dangers. But it was the production of his portfolio called 'The Bottle', in 1847, which startled him into total abstention. He had taken the eight drawings to William Cash, chairman of the National Temperance Society. The gentle Quaker recognised the personal insight in the drawings, and casually asked Cruikshank why, if he could so vividly see what drink does to a man, did he persist in gulping down alcohol himself? From that day, Cruikshank never touched alcohol again, and crusaded zestfully against it. Even on the occasion of his silver wedding, in 1875, when the house in Hampstead Road was crowded with his friends and admirers, it was with tea that the toast to Mr and Mrs Cruikshank was drunk. He was then 85, and died here three years later. The plaque was erected by the Royal Society of Arts in 1885.

In Doughty Street, WC1, are two plaques, one at **14 Doughty Street** to **Sydney Smith**, the author and wit, and the other, at **48 Doughty Street** to **Charles Dickens.** Smith (1771–1845) only lived four years in this house, arriving here from Edinburgh where in 1802 he had founded the famous *Edinburgh Review* with Francis Jeffrey and Henry Brougham. He was aged 32, and with him came his wife. They were so poor that Mrs Smith had to sell a great deal of jewellery given to her by her mother to obtain anywhere to live. With the £500 they received, they were able to settle in this small house in Doughty Street while Smith looked for a preachership. London at that time hardly knew him. Only the readers of the *Edinburgh Review* were familiar with his name. After some time, he found a position at The Foundling Hospital, and his reputation as a speaker began to spread. In 1804, he was invited to lecture at The Royal Institution. 'The lecturer' the *Dictionary of National Biography* tells us 'modestly professed to aim at no more than a popular exposition of

Left: *The exterior of Dickens' House, Doughty Street, WC1, now the headquarters of the worldwide Dickens fellowship and a museum in remembrance of the greatest novelist of the nineteenth century. The museum is open daily to the public.*
Below: *The drawing room at 48 Doughty Street, which was formerly used by Dickens as his dining room. The knob and knocker seen on the door in this photograph were previously on the front door, but were removed inside the house to avoid the attention of over enthusiastic souvenir hunters.*
Right: *A drawing of Charles Dickens made in 1838 by George Cruikshank. The drawing was executed one year after Dickens had moved into his new home in Doughty Street.*

Left: *Charles Dickens. Such was the popularity of Dickens that many caricatures of him appeared in his lifetime.*

"moral philosophy" . . . but the ingenuity and humour of his illustrations and his frequent touches of shrewd morality made them singularly successful.' Albermarle Street was impassable. Galleries had to be added to the lecture hall. 'There was such an uproar', quipped Smith as he 'never remembered to have been excited by any other literary imposture.' The lectures were so successful that Smith was launched in a city which feasted off stylish witticisms and bon mots. He soon became a member of the charmed inner circle, with invitations to all the grand households. The revenue he earned also enabled him to move to a larger residence. The plaque was erected in 1906.

48 Doughty Street, WC1 was the residence of Charles Dickens and his family from 1837 until 1841. Dickens had recently married Catherine Hogarth, daughter of a colleague on the *Morning Chronicle*, the paper for which he had reported the proceedings from the House of Commons for four years. He had recently published too his first major success, *The Pickwick Papers*, so that when their first child was born, a son, they were able to move into this house from their previous accommodation in Furnival's Inn. With them moved Catherine's younger sister, Mary, of whom Dickens said, 'So perfect a creature never breathed. She had not a fault'. 'Mary', wrote Michael and Mollie Hardwick in their *Charles Dickens Companion*, 'was a robust, merry girl, and it was a happy family that inhabited the house which is now the headquarters of the Dickens Fellowship. But the happiness was short lived. One night after returning from the theatre, Mary was taken ill and died the next day. With no previous sign or warning, her light was extinguished all in a moment. . . . Mary's death burnt itself into his mind and branded it for ever. He wore her ring on his finger until his own death, and for years was haunted by a recurrent vision of her. This sorrow is suffered, over and over again, in his books – in the death of Dora in *David Copperfield*, the death of Little Nell in *The Old Curiosity Shop* and the nearly fatal illness of Rose Maylie in *Oliver Twist*. Had she been his wife or his betrothed, his mourning could not have been greater; yet at the time of her death he was a newly married man. . . .' This was a very private grief, and did not outwardly affect how others found him. Certainly he did not change the stylish clothes, for which he was famed. A. St John Adcock writes of him that 'his dress was florid. A satin cravat of the deepest blue, relieved by embroideries, a green waistcoat with gold flowers, a dress coat with a velvet collar, and satin facings, as well as opulence of white cuff, rings in excess, made up rather a striking whole'. Once, when Wilkie Collins had been presented with some brilliant materials for new curtains, he suggested Dickens might like the left-overs to make a new waistcoat.

Dickens was a hard and methodical worker. It was here that *Oliver Twist* was written. The book did not come easily to him. Dickens wrote to his friend Forster 'sitting patiently at home waiting for *Oliver Twist* who has not yet arrived', so that day at least Dickens took none of the hard exercise he found so stimulating and refreshing after a concentrated stint of composition. Frequently Dickens and Forster would go riding or walking together. It was typical of Dickens to write early in the morning to Forster, who lived in Lincoln Inn Fields, suggesting a meeting later on for 'a fifteen mile ride out, ditto in, and lunch on the road, with a wind up dinner in Doughty Street'. On another occasion Dickens sent a note proposing a brisk walk to Hampstead and over the Heath, and, afterwards, at Jack Straw's Castle, 'a red hot chop for dinner, and a glass of good wine'. But when Dickens was wrestling with the story of *Oliver Twist* the letters told a different story and begged: 'Don't, don't let us

Darwin as an elderly man, photographed by Julia Margaret Cameron thirteen years before the great naturalist's death in 1882.

ride till tomorrow, not yet having disposed of the Jew, who is such an out and outer that I don't know what to make of him.' Good friend that he was, Forster used to go to Doughty Street instead and sit with Dickens in his study, quietly reading the manuscript, and answering with comments only when the novelist threw out a sudden thought or suggestion for the direction the story should go. At the end of *Oliver Twist*, Forster sat in the study, talking over the last chapter of the book with Dickens, remaining there and reading quietly while Dickens wrote it. After *Oliver Twist* was finished, Dickens embarked on *Nicholas Nickleby*. 'Dickens had been haunted since childhood', writes Hardwick, 'by a story he had heard about the notorious "Yorkshire Schools": cheap boarding schools run entirely for profit, where unwanted boys, usually illegitimate, were farmed out and kept under miserable conditions.' In 1838, Dickens visited Yorkshire to search out these schools he later caricatured in Dotheboys Hall. Dickens was already house-hunting by the following year. With a growing family and an increasing circle of friends to entertain he was in need of a larger home and anyway the death of Mary in his arms in the bedroom at the top of the stairs, still haunted him frequently. He needed a house whose memories did not come between him and his writing. In 1849, he and his family moved to **Devonshire Terrace, W2,** where he had found a large, handsome house with a garden of considerable size. 48 Doughty Street today is a museum where a fine collection of Dickensiana is on view, including small parts of the manuscript of *Oliver Twist* and *Nicholas Nickleby*. The plaque was erected here in 1903.

Charles Darwin (1809–1882) the naturalist, and another profound influence on nineteenth century thought, is commemorated at **110 Gower Street, WC1,** where he lived from 1839–1842, almost precisely the same period that Dickens occupied his house in Doughty Street. Like Dickens, too, Darwin moved here on his marriage. Darwin's son described the house as '. . . a small, commonplace London house with a drawing room in front, and a small room behind in which they lived. In later years my father used to laugh over the surpassing ugliness of the furniture, carpets, etc. The only redeeming feature was a better garden that most London houses have, a strip as wide as the house and thirty yards long.' Darwin, who was thirty years old when he moved here, enjoyed the garden. It was a pleasant place to sit during the summer and relax after his work on *Coral Reefs* which he had begun before his marriage to his cousin, Emma Wedgwood. 'The book, though a small one, cost me 20 months of hard work as I had to read every book on the islands of the Pacific and to consult many charts. The last proof sheet was corrected on May 6th, 1842.'

Darwin was not a strong man physically. Though he lived until 1882, dying at the age of 73, the rigours of the H.M.S. *Beagle* Expedition, for which he was the official naturalist, 1831–6, had taken its toll. Despite his delicacy of health, and the severity of the London fogs, Darwin was able to write fondly about his residence to a friend in October 1839, and also about the district, saying, 'there is a grandeur about its smoky fogs, and the dull and distant sounds of cabs and coaches; in fact, you may perceive I am becoming a thorough paced Cockney, and I glory in thoughts that I shall be here for the next six months'. In fact, Darwin stayed another two years, before moving away from London to Kent. Appropriately the plaque that commemorates the author of *The Origin of Species* stands on the walls of the **Biological Sciences Building of University College.**

At **2 Gower Street, WC1,** Dame Millicent Fawcett (1847–1929) is commemorated. A leader in the women's suffrage movement, it was her marriage to Henry Fawcett, Professor of Economics at Cambridge and M.P. for Brighton, which brought her into contact with the radical influences of mid-nineteenth century England. Her husband was blind, so it was her work to see that his correspondence was maintained, and that his papers and manuscripts were properly prepared. This secondary education proved of lasting influence to her. Never a militant, she was nevertheless a profoundly formidable champion of women's suffrage.

Another political activist, **Guiseppe Mazzini**, is commemorated at **183 Gower Street, WC1**. He was only in his early twenties when he took lodgings at this house. Though he only lived here for three years, he was very active with the émigré Italian Republican Movement. A frequent visitor to the Rossetti household in nearby Hallam Street, he also worked tirelessly on behalf of other Italians then living in London. Also nearby at **91 Gower Street, WC1**, **George Dance** (1741–1825) the architect is commemorated.

William Butler Yeats (1865–1939) who lived at **18 Woburn Place, WC1**, was also a young man in his early twenties when he first settled on his own in a meagre apartment at this address. On the ground floor of his house lived a cobbler; above him a workman's family; while the attic housed an old pedlar who painted in water colours. Yeats, whose family had already moved to London some years before, had with him a good many books and pictures. There was only a little furniture when the Irish poet moved here, and, says Joseph Hone, Yeats' biographer, a few meagre purchases were made, 'chiefly of things that he could throw away without regret when he became more prosperous'. A charwoman, Mrs Old, looked in three times a week. Yeats, 'unless he was working', Hone wrote of the poet's routine, he would 'be indoors writing until four, when he dressed, and either received visitors or went out to seek literary friends'. When there were no friends about, Yeats took long solitary walks, his tall cloaked figure striding through the Bloomsbury Streets. These excursions were made necessary by Yeats' poor eyesight, since the poet could not afford the strain of sitting at home reading or writing by candlelight. To the other people in Woburn Buildings, Yeats was known as 'the toff what lives in the Buildings'. This, Hone explains, was because he was the only person there who ever received a letter. Since he was not earning very much as a writer in these early days it paid him to take on the pedlar's room as soon as it became vacant, and turn it into a small kitchen, so that he would not have to go out and eat at a nearby cafe or teashop every day. What little income he had he preferred to keep and spend on his Monday night receptions. The people who came to these, Hone tells us '... had to seek his door beside the cobbler's shop ... children swarming around them, before being led up creaking stairs into a large room hung with Blake engravings, some Beardsleys, a Rossetti, and other pictures of pre-Raphaelite character. The windows with blue curtains looked out on the little shops across the way and on a tree or two. On one side of the fireplace was a low settle, Lady Gregory's gift, like the blue curtains. The books were by Morris and Blake ... and against one of the walls was a long chest in which the author left his manuscripts.' Yeats lived here for a short time after his marriage before moving to take up residence in Oxford. The plaque was erected in 1957.

FURTHER NAMES COMMEMORATED IN ST PANCRAS

Henry Mayhew (1812–1887) founder of *Punch* lived at **55 Albany Street, NW1**; **Charles Turner** (1774–1857) the engraver, lived at **56 Warren Street, W1**; **Lord Salisbury** (1830–1903), is remembered at **21 Fitzroy Square, W1**; and **C. Patmore** poet and essayist at **14 Percy Street, W1**.

HAMPSTEAD

Hampstead stands upon one of the highest hills around London. 'On top of the hill indeed', wrote Defoe in lyrical terms, 'there is a very pleasant plain, called the Heath, which on the very summit, is a plain of about a mile every way: and in good weather 'tis pleasant airing upon it, and some of the streets are extended so far, as that they begin to build, even on the highest part of the hill. But it must be confest, 'tis so near heaven, that I dare not say it can be a proper situation, for any but a race of mountaineers, whose lungs have been used to a rarify'd air, nearer the second region, than any ground for 30 miles round it.' And it was not only the air that drew people there. There was also the water of the Wells, 'exceedingly pure spring water, with a faint trace of earthy salts such as those of iron, magnesia and lime'. In 1700 the authorities ordered 'that the spring lyeing by the purging wells be forthwith brot to the toune of Hamsted, as the parish charge, and y^t ye money profitts arising thereout be applied tow^{rds} easing the poor rates hereafter to be made'. Seymour wrote in 1735: 'This village is much more frequented by good company than can well be expected considering its vicinity to London, but such care had been taken to discourage the meaner sort from making it a place of residence that it is now become, after Scarborough and Bath and Tunbridge, one of the politest Public Places in England.'

One of the politest inhabitants of Hampstead was **Joanna Baillie** (1762–1851) the poet and dramatist, who is commemorated by a plaque at **Bolton House, Windmill Hill, NW3**. She is remembered as a girl of 20, in 1782, with her sister 'gathering the gold thorn blazing on the Heath,

and roaming about the old gravel pits and water courses'. Though only a minor literary figure herself, her house became one of the first major literary salons in London. Scott and Wordsworth were both visitors here, and Scott looked forward with pleasure to his journeys to the quiet, picturesque, old fashioned red brick mansion standing on the top of Windmill Hill, though sometimes the return journeys were not so pleasant. He wrote in a letter to her 1811: 'The most dreadful fright I ever had in my life was returning from Hampstead the day which I spent so pleasantly with you. Although the evening was nearly closed, I foolishly chose to take a short cut through the fields, and in the enclosures where the path leads by a thick and high hedge with several gaps. In it, however, did I meet with one of your thorough paced London ruffians – at least, judging from the squalid and jail bird appearance and black-guard expression of countenance . . . I saw no weapon he had except a stick, but as I moved on to gain the stile which was to let me into the free field, with the idea of the wretch springing on me from the cover at every step I took, I assure you I would not wish the worst enemy I ever had to undergo such a feeling as I had for about five minutes.'

Luckily for Walter Scott, he survived this man, who was almost certainly one of the large number of footpads and highwaymen who waylaid travellers on the Heath. Clearly he had had no such experience when, on being asked whether among the poets born north of the Tweed he preferred Burns or Campbell, he declared unequivocally, with no thoughts of the dangerous area in which she lived, 'Joanna Baillie is now the highest genius of our country!' Clearly there was a touch of patronising flattery in this remark, for, although Joanna Baillie was the author of several plays, and although an actress of the calibre of Mrs Siddons was pleased not only to act in it at Drury Lane, but also to make a point of

The home of Joanna Baillie, Bolton House, Windmill Hill in Hampstead. From this commanding position the house looks out on one of the finest views in old Hampstead. Not many yards away in Holly Bush Hill, the house of George Romney stands.

friendship with the dramatist, Joanna Baillie's poetry was little more than derivative, if not imitative of other greater talents who were members of her circle. Wordsworth was amongst them, and he said of her: 'If I had to present to any foreigner any one as a model of an English gentlewoman, it would be Joanna Baillie.' The ubiquitous Crabbe-Robinson states in his journal of May 1812: 'Joined Wordsworth in the Oxford Road (Oxford Street); we got into the fields and walked to Hampstead ... we met Miss Joanna Baillie and accompanied her home. She is small in figure, and her gait is mean and shuffling; but her manners are those of a well-bred lady. She has none of the unpleasant airs too common of literary ladies, even her conversation is pleasant!' In old age, she continued to entertain. G. B. Shaw wrote of her and her sister in the *Dictionary of National Biography*: 'Even when one became an octogenarian and the other a nonegerian they could enter keenly into the various literary and scientific controversies of the day.' Perhaps the most pleasing recollection of her comes from an American visitor, a Miss Sedgwick who wrote: 'Miss Baillie has a well preserved appearance: her face has nothing of the vexed or sorrowful expression that is so often deeply stamped by a long experience of life ... she has a pleasing figure ... She wears her own grey hair, a gentle fashion, by the way, here, which I wish we elderly ladies of America may have the courage and the taste to imitate!' Joanna Baillie died in 1851 at the age of 89.

John Keats (1795–1821) commemorated at **Wentworth Place, Keats Grove, NW3,** enjoyed no such longevity. He died in 1821 from consumption aged just 25. Keats and his two brothers, George and Tom, were left parentless after the death of their mother in 1810. Their father, who had worked at a stable in Finsbury, had died some years before, after a fall from a horse. Keats had left school in 1811, and was apprenticed to a surgeon under whom he started to study at Guy's and St Thomas's Hospital in Southwark. He was not keen on medicine, and already wanted a literary career for himself. By the following year he was seeking out Leigh Hunt, (see page 17) then living in the Vale of Health, Hampstead, and showing him some poems he had written. Leigh Hunt encouraged him, so much so that Keats soon became a frequent visitor here, meeting Shelley, Haydon, Wordsworth, Hazlitt and others. In 1817, he and his two brothers settled in Well Walk at the cottage of Bentley, the postman. It was here that *Endymion* was written. By now Keats had met the two young men Charles Wentworth Dilke and Charles Armitage Brown, who had built a pair of semi-detached houses on the same lovely garden plot of land called Wentworth Place. A friendship was formed, but it was not until the death of Keats' younger brother Tom from consumption that Keats was given the chance to live there. 'Early next morning' writes Brown in December 1818 'I was awakened in bed by a pressure on my hand. It was Keats who had come to tell me that his brother was no more. . . . I said nothing . . . at last, my thoughts returning from the dead to the living, I said, "Have you nothing more to do with those lodgings and alone, too. Had you better not live with me?" He pressed my hand warmly and replied, "I think that would be better." From that moment he was my inmate.'

Living in the other house there was a Mrs Brawne and her daughters, one of whom was Fanny, and with whom Keats fell rapidly in love. Already, anxious over financial worries, and ill himself half the time with an ominously sore throat, the future was presaging itself for Keats. Yet, despite this, the summer of 1819 was a happy one for Keats. Fanny was always in and out of his house, better still she was returning his love. A mark of his contentment is revealed by the superbly lyrical quality of his *Ode To A Nightingale* which was written down in the

HAMPSTEAD 119

Left: *The backs of houses in the Vale of Health seen from one of the several ponds of Hampstead Heath.*
Below: *This portrait of John Keats shows him in his sitting room which can be seen at Keats House, now a museum. It was painted in 1821 by Joseph Stevens who nursed Keats until his death in Italy.*
Bottom left: *This view of Keats House shows the spot at the right where the original plum tree grew under which Keats sat to write 'Ode to a Nightingale', after going out into the garden on hearing a nightingale singing.*

Left: George Romney's house on Holly Bush Hill was bought by the painter for £700 in 1796. Romney had great visions for it and enthusiastically set about tearing down the old stables to build an art gallery and a large studio in their place. But the elderly painter's dream of a home that would revitalise his art never came true. He died only six years later in Kendal.

garden of Wentworth Place. In fact, the signs of his own consumption had been visible for some time. After returning from an exhausting walking tour from Scotland Mrs Brawne had noted that Keats was 'as brown and shabby as you can imagine. I cannot tell you what he looked like'. While, even earlier than that, in the summer of 1816, Coleridge tells us even more pertinently about Keats' condition. Coleridge had come to Hampstead to live with a Mr Gilman, a surgeon, trying to cure himself of the opium habit. He was walking across the common one afternoon with Leigh Hunt on his way back to Highgate where he was staying when they happened to meet Keats. He was, wrote Coleridge '. . . a loose, slack, and not well dressed youth. . . . He was introduced to me and stayed a minute or so. After he had left us a little way, he ran back and said "Let me carry away the memory, Coleridge, of having pressed your hand". "There is death in that hand", I said when Keats was gone; yet this was, I believe, before the consumption showed itself distinctly.'

It was soon to do so. It was February 1820. Keats had been to London, and, with a sudden thaw coming on after very cold weather, had left off his overcoat. Returning to Hampstead, and riding on top of the coach and horses, he had caught a severe chill. When he arrived back at Wentworth Place Brown saw at once that he had a fever, and persuaded him to go to bed. 'He did so immediately', wrote Brown, 'but before his head was on the pillow he coughed slightly and I heard him say "That is blood from my mouth". I went towards him. He was examining a single drop upon the sheet. "Bring me a candle, Brown, and let me see this blood." After regarding it steadfastly, he looked up in my face with a calmness of countenance I can never forget and said, "I know the colour of that blood, it is arterial blood – I cannot be deceived in that colour – that drop of blood is my death warrant – I must die." I ran for a

surgeon; my friend was bled, and at five in the morning I left him after for sometime he had been in a gentle sleep. . . .' Keats' medical training had not deceived him, it was the evidence he must have been suspecting for some time, certainly ever since his brother had died. His time now at Wentworth Place was rationed. He read feverishly, cramming in, as he declared in a letter to one of the family 'Beaumont, and Fletcher, Chaucer and a new work of Tom Moore's'.

He loved Fanny Brawne with even greater energy. For a time he recovered, nursed by Fanny's mother. In the spring of 1820 he was well enough even to go to Haydon's exhibition of 'Christ's Entry Into Jerusalem'. But, at the end of that summer he was told he had to leave for Italy by the doctors. It was the end of the road. Brown accompanied him. They went from Naples to Rome, where, on February 23 1821, Keats died. It was not until 12 years later that Fanny Brawne, to whom Keats had become engaged, married another. Keats' house at Keats Grove is now a museum open to the public.

George Romney's association with his Hampstead home on **Holly Bush Hill, NW3,** began in his sixty-third year. The date was 1797, and he was within five years of his death. Romney was a north countryman. At the age of 27, he had married only to leave his wife and small children shortly afterwards as he came to London to make his way as a painter. It was to be a long parting. Within a few years Romney had started to establish himself as a successful artist. Such was the quality of his work that he was able to command high fees, and the money enabled him to be generous in his maintenance towards his family. The story of Romney's move to Hampstead is one of loneliness and approaching old age. For some time Romney had been living in Cavendish Square. Life was becoming empty and bleak, and he was even losing some of his zest for painting. From here, he wrote to a friend: 'I am going to decline business and wind up my bottom; and then build me a house, which I hope will inspire me with new vigour. . .'

Maxwell, one of Romney's biographers, suggests that: 'Romney had suffered at this time a slight paralytic attack, which temporarily destroyed his perceptive power and artistic expression. . . . Sitters had been sent to flight . . . in their place the artist had surrounded himself with great sheets, on which he was incessantly drawing designs for the new house and gallery on which he had set his heart. . . . His son was only just in time to prevent him signing a contract to purchase four acres of land in the Edgware Road, whereon to build a palace of art . . .' Instead of such a disastrous scheme, surely the stuff that old men's dreams are made of, Romney was persuaded to buy this house in Holly Bush Hill, in Hampstead. The place was then cluttered up with unwanted stables. Still, the price was only £700, so Romney bought it, and set the builders about their task of constructing, as Maxwell tells us 'an ambitious gallery for statuary and paintings with a few living rooms attached'. The building of the house began in the spring of 1797, and on April 18, that year, Romney wrote to his friend William Hayley, the astrologer: 'I hope that I may see you next winter upon the hill at Hampstead, when I hope to have my new mansion throughly dried, fit for your reception and my gratification. . . . My Hampstead house will be very warm and very convenient for every study.' Alas for an old man's dreams, the building was not going at all well, and when he eventually moved to the house he found it, according to Walter Armstrong, 'difficult to accommodate the pictures and studies in every stage of incompleteness which had accumulated about him. They overflowed the house and lined the damp walls of the new arcade, where many were stolen and others destroyed by exposure to the weather'.

The house was miserably damp, and was very far from being either warm or convenient for study. Worse still, Romney found that the experience of a new environment was no way a stimulation to produce fresh work. Instead, he was simply a lonely, old man refusing to come to terms with the passing years. Quite suddenly, without telling anybody, he left the house here in Holly Bush Hill and returned north to his wife, with whom he stayed for the rest of his life. His son, The Rev. John Romney writes: 'The next summer he came to Kendal, where he purchased the place where now I reside. Feeling his infirmities grow upon him, he did not venture to return to Hampstead, but authorised me to see the house at that place. . . .' Maxwell writes of the same impulsive and desperate search for some comfort in his life: 'Alone, imparting to no human being his intention, Romney quitted London for the last time, and travelled to Kendal to the wife he had left there many years before, who, in those last dark days, resumed her place as his helpmate.' Romney died at home in 1802.

John Galsworthy (1867–1933) commemorated at **Grove Lodge, Hampstead, NW3,** where he lived from 1920 to the end of his life 13 years later, was an altogether much more contented man. R. H. Mottram described him as '. . . athletic looking and rather tanned, just under six feet, but so well proportioned that he looked taller. He was fair, and bluish grey of eye, with long fingered, powerful hands, and a disarming smile'. The house '. . . was a 17th century building, sometime rectory and once inhabited by John Constable. . . . The front door gave upon the corridor as usual in such "cottages" out of which opened successively three rooms looking west into the garden, which Ada (his wife) made into respectively dining room, study and her drawing room. The latter had a bay added and incorporated what had been a little back yard, so that it was pleasantly unusual, caught any sun, and held her piano under a skylight.'

Left: *John Galsworthy's house, Grove Lodge, is seen on the left and adjacent to it is George Gilbert Scott's taller house with its weatherboarding and admiral's platform.*

With the piano housed next door, Galsworthy used to love to hear his wife play something while he was correcting proofs, or browsing over the finished manuscript. He would even, writes Mottram, 'call "play something" when he wrestled with some knotty passage her music would liquefy'. Galsworthy was the least pretentious of men. He was fond of riding or walking after lunch, already having completed a morning's work, and would not take up his pen again until after tea. 'Don't yearn for the literary life', he used to exclaim. 'That's nothing. What you write is what matters!' He was 65 years of age when Mottram saw him for the last time. Mottram was staying at Grove Lodge to go on from there to attend a Royal Literary Fund banquet. 'But on this occasion, coming down dressed, I found that he and Ada were not going. He laughed, tweaked my scarf straight, and sent me off to enjoy a good dinner for them. I did. Next morning, as I left to catch my early train, he came running down in his dressing gown, wrung my hand with "God Bless you, Old Man!" which I did not realise was no conventional phrase, but a parting benediction.' In seven months he was dead.

John Constable (1776–1837) is commemorated at **40 Well Walk, NW3**. Of the house, a modest brick building, he wrote in 1820: 'I have settled in a comfortable house in Well Walk – so hateful is moving about to me that I could gladly exclaim "here let me take my everlasting rest". This house is to my wife's heart's content. It is situated on an eminence at the back, and our little drawing room commands a view unsurpassed in Europe from Westminster Abbey to Gravesend.' He had been living previously in Charlotte Street, but had rented out his house there to bring his sick wife to the better air in Hampstead. Like Keats, she was tubercular, and had only a short time to live. Constable, of course, knew Hampstead well. He had been to the secluded village many times, taking his sketchpad and paints with him. Of Hampstead he had said: 'I love every stile, and stump, and lane in the village; as long as I am able to hold a brush I shall never cease to paint them.' But now the summer days spent outside no longer held the same attraction. There was always the moment when he had to return home and witness again the pitiably brave attempts of his wife to appear well and cheerful as she greeted him. Sometimes, when Constable painted at home, and she lay on the sofa nearby, and visitors called, Constable used to burst into tears at their pretence that everything was normal in the house. Kind Dr Evans, looking after Constable's rheumatics, could do little to help. Their only real pleasures together came from the children, being looked after by the conscientious Miss Noble, and the occasional gathering of friends after some fresh venison had been sent up from Ham by one of Constable's admirers. Mrs Constable died in November 1828, and John and the children continued to live in Well Walk for a period before returning to Charlotte Street. Also commemorated in **Well Walk** is **Henry Hyndman** (1842–1921) the socialist leader. He lived at No. 13.

Sir Walter Besant (1836–1901) commemorated at **Frognal End, Frognal Gardens, NW3,** exemplified the twin ideals of scholarship and philanthropy so typical of the well-to-do in the mid and late-Victorian era. Besant today is remembered for his immensely readable volumes about the history of London. In his lifetime, however, it was much more his services to the poor and needy for which he was known. This was not armchair philanthropy, but based on first hand experiences during his researching for two novels *All Sorts and Conditions of Men* (1882) and *Children of Gideon*, in which he advocated definite proposals for the evils and deprivations he had encountered in London's East End. On the fanlight of his study in his Hampstead home were written the words 'Work while it is day, for the night cometh

Below left: *A self-portrait of John Constable.*
Below right: *John Constable's house in Well Walk, Hampstead, stands opposite the ornate stone sculptured well that surrounds the natural water spring which gave this thoroughfare its name.*

when no man can work'. Besant followed the sense in the quotation. He did not merely advocate, he made it his business that some of his suggestions became reality. The provision of better recreational facilities to London's poor was an abiding interest, and it was largely due to his inspiration that the 'People's Palace' was opened by Queen Victoria in May 1887 in the Mile End Road. Besant, as he revealed in his autobiography, spent remarkably little time in his house in Hampstead and it featured only sparsely in the great advents of his life. He was a great club man; very active on local historical committees in Hampstead, as well as being a moving light behind The Society of Authors, which, with Tennyson as President, he and 12 others founded in 1884. In George Meredith's words Besant was 'a valorous, alert, persistent advocate of the author's cause and sought to establish a system of fair dealing between the sagacious publishers of books and the inexperienced, often heedless producers'. Besant was a thick set figure, with a bushy beard, and somewhat brusque in manner, but genial among intimate friends and always ready to help aspiring writers. His greatest work *A Survey of Modern London* was started in 1894, and he died at home in 1901.

Though **Samuel Taylor Coleridge** (1792–1834) is commemorated at **7 Addison Bridge Road, W6**, in Fulham, it was here in Hampstead that he spent the last, and in some ways, most contented years of his life. Like Constable, he suffered badly from rheumatism, and had started, foolishly early on in his short life, to kill the pain by taking laudanum. For a while his life started to fragment, and his writing suffered too. It was a chance meeting with Dr Gillman that offered him the opportunity to rid himself of this dreadful addiction. The Gillmans were childless, and readily took Coleridge into their home, at **3 The Grove, Highgate, N6**, where a stone plaque exists to commemorate the poet's stay. Coleridge was

just 24, and the date was 1816. 'Coleridge's room', records A. Howitt, 'looked upon a delicious prospect of wood and meadow, with a gay garden full of colour under the window. When a friend of his first saw him there, he said he thought he had taken to his dwelling place like an abbot. There he cultivated his flowers, and had a set of birds for his pensioners, who came to breakfast. . . . He might be seen taking his daily stroll up and down near Highgate, with his black coat and white locks and a book in his hand, and was a great acquaintance of the little children.' Coleridge was a superb conversationalist, and the Gillmans' drawing room, which opened out onto a terrace, with a flight of stone steps descending to the lawns, was the scene of many soirées where the poet held his audience of guests enraptured. Thomas Dibdin, writing in 1828, remembers such an occasion: 'I shall never forget the effect his first conversation made upon me at the first meeting. . . . It struck me as something not only out of the ordinary course of things, but as an intellectual exhibition altogether matchless. . . . The party was unusually large, but the presence of Coleridge concentrated all attention towards himself. The viands were unusually costly, and the banquet was at once rich and varied; but there seemed to be no dish like Coleridge's conversation to feed upon. . . . For nearly two hours he spoke with unhesitating and uninterrupted fluency. As I returned homeward, I thought a 2nd Dr Johnson had visited the earth to make wise the sons of men. . . .' Coleridge died here in 1834, aged 42.

George Gilbert Scott (1811–1878) the architect, is commemorated at **21 Hampstead Grove, NW3**, where he and his family moved in 1856. Two main commissions were occupying him professionally at this time, the erection of the Foreign and India Office in Whitehall, and the preparation of The Albert Memorial. The latter he felt very trying, since his ideas and

Left: *A portrait of William Friese-Greene whose plaque is shown being erected in 1954 on page 6.*
Top right: *A photographic portrait of the pioneer psychoanalyst Sigmund Freud, taken in his later years.*
Bottom right: *A portrait of D. H. Lawrence in his late twenties.*

designs were constantly at the mercy of committees of grave faced Victorian worthies appointed to erect a suitably magnificent memorial to the Queen's beloved late husband.

Alfred Stevens (1817–1875) the artist and sculptor, commemorated at **9 Eton Villas, NW3,** was beset by similar problems. His main commission was the Wellington monument in St Paul's Cathedral. Once again, he found his ideas ever being modified and changed by his sponsors. Stevens was 40 when he was entrusted with this work in 1857. The commission was to occupy him for the rest of his life. Possibly one of the difficulties he faced was a satisfactory way of communicating with the élite of the military, political and artistic establishment who would eventually choose the right design for Wellington's monument. Stevens was a very private man. Dorset born, he came from humble stock, being educated at the local village school, and working with his father for a number of years as a painter and decorator. W. J. Linton wrote of Stevens: 'He was so engrossed with work that he never went into society. It was difficult to drag him out even to dine with his friend Wehnert's family. . . . I have known him turn his back when, as the door was opened, he saw an extra hat in the hall, with "O Wehnert! I forgot!" – that there was something to prevent his stay, and we had almost to force him in. He was incessantly at his work. I have gone in upon him at 10 o'clock in the morning. "What, breakfasting so late as this?" "My dear fellow, I breakfasted at 4 o'clock. This is my lunch!"' Stevens' only recreation was to go away yachting with some friends for a few days, or to read magazines. These he loved, and friends used to present him with large piles of back numbers, whence he would disappear sometimes for as long as two to three days at a time, to devour them greedily. A bachelor, he was of middle height, and was always very neat and exact in his dress. Sometimes he was taken for a Catholic

priest by those who did not know him. While working, he frequently carried a small dog in the breast pocket of his coat, and allowed peacocks to strut around in his studio.

Gerald du Maurier (1873–1943) the actor manager, is commemorated at **14 Cannon Place, NW3; George du Maurier,** the artist and writer has a plaque at **New Grove House,** in **Hampstead Grove, NW3.**

Two names synonymous with psychiatry and photography respectively had associations with Hampstead. **Sigmund Freud** the psychoanalyst lived briefly at **20 Maresfield Gardens, NW3,** the year before his death here in 1939; and **William Friese-Greene** (1855–1921) the pioneer of cinematography, is commemorated at **136 Maida Vale, NW8.**

The Vale of Health in Hampstead, a small cluster of elegant houses, shrouded from the main road by protective slopes, is a tiny hamlet hidden amongst the trees and ponds of the Heath. Here Leigh Hunt once lived; here Constable stood with his easel, and Keats composed some of his most affectionate verse to the neighbourhood. It was here, too, years later, in the summer of 1915 that **D. H. Lawrence** and his wife Freida came to live at **1 Byron Villas, Vale of Health, NW3.** Lawrence lived first in the London area in Croydon, where, in October 1908, he had started teaching at The Davidson Road School. Lawrence was then in his early twenties. He was to stay teaching there for over four years. At that time he was living with the Jones family, staying with them at No. 12 and 16 Colworth Road. These, Harry T. Moore writes in his biography of Lawrence, *The Intelligent Heart*, 'are identical houses set behind low brick walls, the ground floor walled in red brick, the storey above in rough cement, the gabled roofs shingled, drainpipes and sometimes electric wires going down the outside of the houses'. Mr Jones was a Lancastrian, and a school attendance officer. Lawrence had a walk of about three quarters of a mile from the house to the school, where, according to Moore

'he was a success with both pupils and staff'. A fellow teacher A. W. McLeod recalled something of the school. 'The school was large, the rooms spacious, well lighted and warmed. The staff was good and the common rooms comfortable. The environment was not inspiring . . . The outlook was particularly repellant to Lawrence, who wrote:

'I pick my̆ way over threadbare grass,
   which is pressed
Into mud – the space fast shrinks in the
   builder's hands'.'

McLeod also testifies that Lawrence 'was intolerant of authority' while 'the routine of life was . . . abhorrent'. There is an amusing story from the same source, quoted in Moore's book, about Lawrence's art teaching which, McLeod says '. . . was somewhat suspect. While I was conferring with a Board of Education Inspector', he writes, 'a boy brought a large pastel drawing, still life, for inspection. After a glance I made an ineffectual attempt to suppress the sketch. The official eye had, however, anticipated my effort. "Is this sent for any particular reason?" I inquired. "Mr Lawrence thought it was rather good", the boy replied. The artist returned to his class leaving the masterpiece with us.

"Are you by any chance an artist?" inquired the wary dictator. "No", I replied. "Neither am I", he commented. "We had better be careful about this man. After the session, without his knowledge, collect a sample of these drawings. I will send them to the Art Department at Kensington for an expert opinion". Later they were returned by the Inspector in person. "Good thing we took the course we did", he reported. "The department highly approves. You'll have a crowd of students down to worry you about them, I expect!"'

Lawrence was already writing, and in the summer of 1909, the first of his work was sent to Ford Madox Ford, editor of the *English Review*. 'Its first paragraph', Moore writes about the

Odour of Chrysanthemums, the story which had been sent, 'indicated to Ford that Lawrence was a skilled writer; he at once put it into the basket reserved for accepted manuscripts'. Gradually, through these early associations with Ford, Lawrence began to make an entrée into a literary circle that included Ezra Pound; Galsworthy; G. Lowes Dickinson and G. P. Gooch. As Moore observes, 'No young schoolmaster up from the Midlands could have made a more auspicious debut'.

H. T. Moore recorded Lawrence's early visit to Hampstead when he attended a literary party at the house of Ernest Rhys, first editor of *Everyman's Library*. Ford, Pound and Yeats were there also. After supper, everyone began reading their poems, and it was: 'after Ford had spoken a bright little parody that Ernest Rhys asked the quiet young man to read some of his poems. Lawrence "rose nervously but very deliberately, walked across to a writing desk whose lid was closed, opened it, produced a mysterious book out of his pocket, and sat down, his back to the company, and began to read in an expressive, not very audible voice". The older poets waited politely for him to finish. But after a while it became doubtful if he would finish. Still keeping his back to them, still reading in a low voice, he turned page after page of his notebook and went through poem after poem. At the end of a half an hour the room was full of murmuring: this did not disturb Lawrence who went on reading in his barely audible tone. Finally, at the suggestion of one of the women, Rhys went over to Lawrence and said that he must need a little rest: why not stop for a while now and begin again at midnight?' When Lawrence came to live in Hampstead some years later he was married, and much more self assured. It was in the summer of 1915 that he and Freida moved into the ground floor flat at **1 Byron Villas**, Vale of Health. Mr Moore quotes Christopher Hassall, the poet, who once lived nearby as describing Byron Villas in a letter as 'an ugly little red brick building about fifty years old, with Victorian bow-windows, and frosted glass in the front door'. During his brief stay here, Lawrence was trying to set up a new critical magazine called *Signature* together with his friend, Middleton Murry. A cheap office was found in Red Lion Square, a few meetings were held between literary friends, and the magazine made a brief appearance before it folded. **Middleton Murry** and **Katherine Mansfield**, with whom he was living, are commemorated at **17 East Heath Road, NW3**, nearby to the Vale of Health. They used to join the Lawrences for picnics on the Heath that summer, but were not present on the night of September 8 1915, when Lawrence and Freida were strolling across the slopes that look down towards central London. It was the occasion of the first big Zeppelin attack on London. 'Guns boomed and searchlights raked the sky, and a fire burned far off in the City', Lawrence recalled, before including the incident in his novel *Kangaroo* seven years later. But Lawrence was violently against war, and was yearning to leave England. For a time his thoughts turned to America, but by the end of the year he and Freida had settled for Cornwall.

Also commemorated in the Vale of Health are **Rabindranath Tagore**, the Indian poet, who lived in 1861 at No. 3, and **Barbara and J. L. Hammond**, the social historians, who lived at **Hollycot**. **Sir Flinders Petrie**, the Egyptologist, is commemorated at **5 Cannon Place, NW3**; **Kate Greenaway** (1846–1901) the artist, at **39 Frognal, NW3**; the musicians **Dame Clara Butt** (1873–1937) and **Sir Henry Wood** (1869–1944) at **7 Harley Road, NW3** and **4 Elsworthy Road, NW3** respectively; and **Baron Freidrich Von Hügel** (1852–1925) the philosopher and theologian at **4 Holdford Road, NW3**. **Ramsay Macdonald**, (1866–1925) Socialist Prime Minister is commemorated at **9 Howitt Road, NW3**.

BETHNAL GREEN

Israel Zangwill, the writer and philanthropist, who is commemorated at **288 Old Ford Road, E2,** was one of the very first novelists who gave the real Jew to the world 'revealing him', the *Dictionary of National Biography* says, 'as he had never been revealed before, minimising nothing, exaggerating nothing, handling him with profound knowledge and great affection but also with justice'. Zangwill's father was a Russian refugee who had come to London in 1848 to escape the Jewish child conscription policy instituted by the Tsar. Israel was born sixteen years later. He went to the Jewish Free School in Spitalfields, and to London University. After teaching for a time, he started writing in 1888. He was a witty, elegant writer, and his best known work is *The Children of The Ghetto*. In addition, he was a tireless worker in the Jewish cause. He died in 1926.

FINSBURY

At **47 City Road, EC1**, John Wesley is commemorated. Born in 1703, it was not until 1778 that the founder of Methodism was able to move into his new London headquarters. In March of 1775 he wrote to his brother Charles, 'On Friday I hope to be in London and to talk to the committee about building a new foundery'. The permission was granted, and the new chapel was opened in November 1778. Wesley's house, however, was not ready until the following year. His apartment was on the first floor, while several other younger clergy lodged there in the house with him. This smart new house attracted a great deal of attention in the area, including some from thieves. In his journal for November 1784, Wesley records: 'At three o'clock in the morning two or three men broke into our house through the kitchen window. Thence they came up into the parlour and broke open Mr Moore's bureau. They next broke open the cupboard, and took away some silver spoons. . . . Just at this time, the alarum, which Mr Moore, by mistake, had set for half past three instead of four o'clock, went off, as it usually did, with a thundering noise. At this the thieves ran away with all speed tho' half their work was not done.' The thieves were not the only ones in trouble in the house, as Wesley records another day in his journal. 'I went down at 5.30 but found no preacher in chapel, though we had three or four in the house, so I preached myself. Afterwards, inquiring why none of my family attended the morning preaching, they said it was that they sat up too late. I resolved to put a stop to this, and therefore ordered that (1) everyone under my roof should go to bed at 9 p.m. that (2) everyone might attend the morning preaching.'

Not all was solemn ritual in this house, however, and especially when his brother Charles, the hymn writer, visited there. 'Not infrequently', writes Henry Moore in his *Life of Wesley* 'having left the pony in the garden he would enter, crying out "Pen and Ink! Pen and Ink!" These being supplied he wrote the hymn he had been composing. When this was done he would look round on those present, and salute them with much kindness, ask after their health, give out a short hymn, and thus put all in mind of eternity.' Wesley died here, in March 1791, as Samuel Rodgers, who was returning home to Stoke Newington from a business meeting, and passing the house in City Road, records 'I saw a number of respectable persons of both sexes assembled here, all well dressed in mourning, and with very serious look and behaviour. The door of the house was open and they entered in pairs. I thought that, without impropriety, I might join them, so we all walked upstairs, and came to a drawing room in the midst of which was a table; on this table lay the body of a person dressed in a clergyman's robes, with bands, and his grey hair shading his face on either side. He was of small stature, and his countenance looked like wax. After we had gone round the table in our lingering procession, we descended downstairs. The person that lay before us was the celebrated John Wesley, and at the earnest request of his congregation they were permitted to take this pathetic and affectionate farewell of their beloved pastor.'

Also commemorated in Finsbury is **William Caslon** (1692–1766) typefounder, at **23 Chiswell Street, EC1.**

At **95 Stoke Newington Church Street, N16,** a house used to stand on this site where **Daniel Defoe** lived from 1709 to 1729. The house was a large, and very plain brick mansion with twelve windows, and a walled garden of four acres behind, where Defoe loved to stroll. The house was full of strange cupboards and there were many formidable locks and bars guarding these places where the author's papers and manuscripts were stored. Defoe had good reason to value his privacy. Not only was he a dissenting author whose views the State did not like, and who had already been fined, imprisoned and pilloried, but he had also, as recently as two years before his move into this house, been working as a spy for the Scots, and his clashes with authority were by no means over. By all accounts devious and shifting in his politics, there was equal unanimity that in his private and social life he was kind, considerate and humane. *Robinson Crusoe* was written here.

In **Shoreditch**, at a site in **Curtain Road, EC2,** a plaque commemorates a building which, from 1577–1598, was the first purpose built theatre in London. The site was also once the precinct of the Priory of St John The Baptist, Holywell.

STEPNEY

In **Stepney, E1** the explorers **Willoughby, Borough** and **Frobisher** are commemorated in a memorial in **King Edward Park, Shadwell.** From this reach in the Thames they and other navigators set sail in the latter half of the sixteenth century to explore the Northern Seas. **Captain Cook** (1728–1778) the explorer, lived briefly at **88 Mile End Road, E1.**

In 1866, at a building on the site of **58 Solent House, Ben Jonson Road, E1,** Dr Thomas John Barnardo began his work for children. Born in Dublin in 1845, he had studied medicine at the nearby London Hospital with the intention of becoming a missionary in China. During the time he was a student, he had joined the Ernest St Ragged School, eventually becoming its Superintendent. His work took him through some of the most notorious slums of the East End. But it was the helplessness of the people during the murderous cholera epidemic of 1866 that persuaded him to stay in England rather than to leave for China. The plight of the children disturbed him especially. It was the following year, 1867, that Barnardo made his first positive move to help them. He had been accosted for help by Jim Jarvis, a hatless, shirtless street Arab who had nothing but a few rags to cover him. On inquiring about his home, Barnardo was taken to see, as he himself later recorded, 'a group of eleven poor boys of ages varying from 9 to 18, sleeping in all postures in the gutters of an iron roof, clad in thin rags with not a shred to cover them, exposed under the open sky to all winds and weathers, a spectacle to angels and to men and enough to break any heart of love'. Soon Barnardo had opened an evening school. It met four times a week, and its activities included

Left: Gandhi arriving at 10 Downing Street in November 1931 for talks with Ramsay Macdonald, the Prime Minister.
Below: Gandhi, surrounded by East End admirers, arrives in Canning Town for his meeting with Charles Chaplin. The date was September 22 1931.

readings aloud of *The Pilgrim's Progress* and *Uncle Tom's Cabin* to the three hundred boys who immediately crowded in for the warmth, shelter, and occasional treats of extra food. Barnardo wrote 30 years later: 'Were children so closely packed, I wonder, in any room before or since? I doubt it! I was wedged up. "Teacher, they're squeezing me" calls out one. Another says, "Teacher, I cannot breave". Nor was this much of an exaggeration, for I could hardly "breave" myself.' The first Dr Barnardo's home was opened in 1870, under the patronage of Lord Shaftesbury. By the time of his death in 1905, at the age of 60, Barnardo had rescued and trained almost 60,000 children.

Mary Hughes (1860–1941) who complemented much of Barnardo's work as she ministered to the East End's poor is remembered at **71 Vallance Road, Stepney, E2. Charles Bradlaugh** (1833–1891) advocate of free thought, lived at **29 Turner Street, Stepney, E16.**

POPLAR

Only one plaque rests in Poplar, East London, and that commemorates **Mahatma Gandhi's** stay at **Kingsley Hall, Powis Road, E3,** during his visit to London in 1931. Charles Chaplin went to see Gandhi there, and writes of the meeting in *My Autobiography*: 'I thought his visit to London was a mistake. His legendary significance evaporated in the London scene, and his religious display fell short of impressiveness. In the cold dank climate of England, wearing his traditional loin-cloth, which he gathered about him in disorderly fashion, he seemed incongruous. . . . I met him in a humble little house in the slum district off the East India Dock Road. Crowds filled the streets and the Press and photographers packed both floors. The interview took place in an upstairs front

room about twelve feet square. The Mahatma had not yet arrived; and as I waited I began to think of what I would say to him. I had heard of his imprisonment and hunger strikes, and his fight for the freedom of India, and vaguely knew of his opposition to machinery. When at last he arrived there was hooraying and cheering as he stepped out of the taxi, gathering about him the folds of his loin cloth. It was a strange scene in that crowded little slum street, that alien figure entering a humble house, accompanied by cheering throngs.'

After posing for their photographs before the Press, Chaplin and Gandhi talked. Of their conversation, Chaplin writes: 'I got a lucid lesson in tactical manoeuvring in India's fight for freedom, inspired, paradoxically, by a realistic, virile minded visionary with a will of iron to carry it out. He also told me that supreme independence is to shed oneself of unnecessary things, and that violence eventually destroys itself. When the room cleared, he asked me if I would like to remain and see them at prayers. The Mahatma sat cross-legged on the floor while five others sat in a circle with him. It was a curious sight: six figures squatting on the floor in that small room, in the heart of the London slums, as a saffron sun was rapidly sinking behind the roof tops, and myself sitting on a sofa looking down at them, while they humbly intoned their prayer.' The plaque to Gandhi was erected in 1954.

SOUTH OF

THE RIVER

BATTERSEA

Battersea lies directly south of the Thames at Chelsea Reach and extends to the perimeter of Clapham Common. It is here, at **110 North Side, SW18** that **John Burns** P.C., M.P., is commemorated. Burns, who lived from 1858–1943, was described by one columnist, as: 'The Hereward the Wake of Modern Politics, who gleefully whirls his gleaming battle axe of invective over the idle, the slack, the worthless and the corrupt in high places and low.' He was born in South Lambeth, effectively part of Battersea, and continued to live in the area for the whole of his life. 'From Candle Factory to British Cabinet' was how a 1908 biography headlined his life story, and indeed this single slogan neatly capsulates the career of one of London's most devoted, and single-minded public servants. The Battersea into which he was born was a thriving suburb of artisan dwellings and small shops. He described a little of his early childhood when, years later, he was fighting for better housing for his constituents. He had just been to look over a damp and filthy tenement. 'It was in a basement like this that I had to spend a good deal of my time as a lad. In one corner the boots were cleaned; in another corner I slept. Now you understand my opposition to basement houses.' As ever, his oratory was straightforward, simple and direct. At the age of ten John Burns, who came of Scottish stock, went to work in Price's Candle Factory where he earned only a few pennies a week. He soon showed his mettle, and his ready fist left its mark on many a bully's face. Always well looked after by his mother, it was her determination that took Burns away from the factory to receive proper schooling at an establishment attached to The Church of St

Mary's, Battersea. Fed on a strict diet of porridge and broth, he grew up to be both stronger and fitter than many in the more pampered houses across the river in smart Chelsea.

Burns did well at school. He left with enough education to move into responsible employment as an engineering hand. He was already active in politics, speaking from an upturned lemonade box in Battersea Park, where, on a Sunday, he played many a good game of cricket. For two years he was out of the country, as a foreman engineer at Akassa, West Africa. Resolute and with a cool head he showed his determination on more than one occasion, rescuing a companion from the grips of a large snake, and diving into a shark infested creek to rescue the lost blade of a propeller. But this was but a temporary diversion from his burning interest – the welfare of his fellow Londoners. He was soon back in Battersea again, campaigning on Clapham Common for a more just society. It was at this time that British Socialism, dormant since the failure of Chartism almost thirty years before, was beginning to re-assert itself. A prime cause in this movement was the arrival in Britain of political refugees from France and Germany. Burns was in touch with them. He also read extensively. He was steeling himself for the moment when he could make his own assault on the political establishment at Westminster and effect change in the lives of those about him. In 1886, after the riots following The National Dock Strike, Burns was tagged 'The Man With The Red Flag'. He had been one of the ringleaders behind a mass rally held in Trafalgar Square. The rally had turned into a riot. Many windows were smashed in the clubs of Pall Mall. Horses and their carriages bolted in terror as the angry dockers expressed their pent up fury at their working and living conditions. As for Burns, he was arrested, but so eloquently did he defend himself at his subsequent trial at the Old Bailey that he was released, his reputation enormously enhanced by his superb oratory from the dock. Burns' trial was within two years of one of London's most significant developments ever – the establishment in 1888 of the London County Council. This was Burns' opportunity – the one he had been waiting for. Offering himself for election, a typical saying of his from the platform was: 'High hats and frock coats have had their day. Now it is time for corduroy and fustian to have their innings.' Burns was to be at the centre of politics for a long time, both as one of the most revered members of the new L.C.C., and as one of the elders of the House of Commons, to which he was soon elected also. He continued to be involved in active politics for many years, and his achievements were many. In his private life he was a devoted husband, and, not surprisingly for such a well read man, an avid collector of books. At the end of his career, his house on North Side contained over 12,000 volumes, including many fine first editions, and a superb collection of works about London.

Burns himself, after his retirement from active politics, became no mean author, with London always his subject. He was very fond of the Thames and its romance. He was once asked, somewhat derisively, by a visiting Canadian and American for a comparison between the Thames and the great rivers of their own countries, the St Lawrence, and the Great Missouri respectively. Without hesitation, Burns replied: 'The St Lawrence is mere water; the Missouri muddy water; but the Thames, my friends, the Thames is liquid History!' He died in 1943, a few weeks after receiving concussion from an exploding German bomb near to his home.

Another campaigner commemorated in Battersea is **William Wilberforce**, who, at the time of his triumph with the anti-slavery campaign, in 1807, was living in a house on the site of **111 Broomwood Road, SW11**. The elegant plaque on the walls of the present building says: 'On the site of this house stood until 1904 Broomwood House (formerly Broomfield) where William Wilberforce resided during the campaign against slavery which he successfully conducted in Parliament.' In the following year Wilberforce went to live in Kensington. There could be no greater contrast to these two men than the burly figure, with a bluff face, enormous chest and full beard, who is commemorated at **33 Lavender Gardens, SW11**. This is **George Henty**, once described as 'The Edgar Wallace of the juvenile story'. Born in 1832, this buccaneer and adventurer and war correspondent for *The Standard*, for which he reported all the major colonial and European wars between 1866 and 1876, was aptly described by Kipling as being 'sent out when a war begins to minister to the blind, brutal, British public's bestial thirst for blood'. Henty was not a malicious man, but he was not in any sense a sensitive one either. A yarn was a good yarn, and there was no sense in worrying about the moralities of imperialism or colonialism. He returned from his travels abroad and embarked on a new career as a writer of children's books in which, generally speaking, the white man was good, and everybody else was not. His books, which he produced at a prolific rate, were enormously popular. Little can be said about his stay here in Battersea. When he was not working, it was generally towards the clubs of the West End that he ventured. It is recorded, however, that his small and cluttered study looked more at times like the corner of some museum than the work place of a busy writer, but then the Ashanti spears hanging on the walls across an old shield, and the crocodile's head propped up in the corner behind a growing pile of old manuscripts were exactly the stuff that his stories were made of, and old men need dreams. His only hobby was sailing, and it was on his yacht, in the autumn of 1902, that he died aged 70. He was buried in Brompton Cemetery.

The final two plaques in Battersea are in commemoration of Edward Thomas and Edward Wilson, both young men who died before their time. **Edward Thomas** lived at **61 Shelgate Road, SW11**, a dour, scowling house to which the poet moved only a few years before he was killed at the front in France in 1917. Thomas and his wife were desperately poor. 'Sensitive and shy, he guarded himself from the world by a fine dry irony.' He had only just achieved recognition from other poets when he moved to Battersea from the Weald in Kent. It is uncertain why he moved to this house. He needed somewhere closer to London for all the literary hack work he was doing. The strain, and indeed the expense of travelling, had been considerable. Perhaps he chose this area because he had been born in Lambeth some 30 years before in 1878. Here, in Battersea, Thomas was doing the most menial work for the greedy and careless editors. He was being paid a mere £1 for every thousand words he wrote. The sheer strain of this once more told on his health, especially as he felt himself imprisoned on a moving staircase of employment which he dare not let go for fear of no money coming in to feed the family.

Walter de la Mare, W. H. Hudson, W. H. Davies and Edward Garnett were all his friends, and indeed admirers. In a sense the First World War came just at the right and at the wrong time for Edward Thomas. It was the right time because it gave him the chance to escape the dreadful impasse into which his life had seemingly drifted; it was the wrong time because, without this excuse, he would surely have surmounted these temporary difficulties himself, and gone on to recapture the zest he had shown in some of his earlier poems, and indeed, in the quality of his biographical work, such as his book on Richard Jeffries (1909). This is borne out by the depth and style of the poetry he started writing once he was at the front. On hearing of his death at Arras, in April of 1917, de la Mare wrote: 'When indeed Edward Thomas was killed at Flanders, a mirror of England was shattered, of so true and pure a crystal that a clearer and tenderer reflection can be found in no other than in these poems.' He died aged only 39 years.

Edward Wilson, born six years earlier than Thomas in 1872, is commemorated at **Battersea Vicarage, 42 Vicarage Crescent, SW11**, in the Thameside village of Battersea. As a young, newly qualified doctor of 26, with an education of Cambridge and St George's Medical School behind him, Wilson came to Battersea to work at the Caius College Mission, one of the many university settlements in the poorer parts of London. In his diary of November 5 1896, he records, 'Packed everything into a four wheeler and came down to live at Caius House, Battersea', adding, somewhat pretentiously, 'living in Battersea is really a good healthy change for me, as I hate society'. In fact, he did not hate society at all. He was an immensely private man, but with a strong sense of duty to others–a contradiction many from a solid middle class background have experienced, and learned to live with. Wilson's way of realising himself was to take his abilities as a surgeon and zoologist into the totally private world of exploring, and in particular Antarctic expeditions. Teaming up with **Robert Falcon Scott** (commemorated at **56 Oakley Street, SW3**) he paid his first visit to the wastes of frozen seas between 1901 and 1904. On that expedition, with Scott and **Shackleton** (also commemorated in London, this time at **12 Westwood Hill, Lewisham, SE26**) he journeyed the farthest south any man had ever penetrated before in the quest for the South Pole. On his return to England, already something of a hero, he substantiated his talents by producing a superbly prepared and illustrated monograph of the mammals and birds he had observed on the trip. Such was his reliability on that first trip that Scott had no hesitation in inviting him to join the next, fatal, expedition, which set sail in 1910.

Below: *A far cry from the icy wastes, this statue of Captain Scott stands in the heart of London, on the east side of Waterloo Place, SW1.*
Left: *Captain Scott leads a sleigh party from his ill-fated expedition over the ice.*

WANDSWORTH

On the walls of the house standing at **11 Putney Hill, SW15** there is a plaque commemorating the residence of the poet **Charles Swinburne** (1837–1909) and his friend **Theodore Walter Watts-Dunton** (1832–1914) the novelist and critic. For a number of years previously Swinburne had been living, on intimate terms, with **Rossetti** at **16 Cheyne Walk** (pages 21, 85, 86, 93). Rossetti, 11 years older than Swinburne, kept a strange household. He had established himself there (the house is also marked by a plaque) in 1862 after the death of his wife. They had only been married two years, and even her death was a bizarre affair. Rossetti had come into the room where her body lay, holding the manuscript of a little book of poems. These he had spoken aloud to her as though she was listening to them. After he had finished, he placed the volume on her hair, and it was buried with her in Highgate Cemetry. Seven years after, by which time he was living at Cheyne Walk, through the pressure of friends, Rossetti gave his consent to have the book exhumed, and it was published with additions in 1870 as the *Lost Poems*. By this time Swinburne and George Meredith were living with Rossetti at Chelsea. Rossetti was deeply attached to Swinburne, and his influence over him was profound. There were those, Watts-Dunton among them, who thought Rossetti's influence too profound.

Life at Cheyne Walk was certainly fun. Whistler and William Morris were constantly in and out of the place, and the rooms were ever changing as Rossetti's mania for collecting curious objects continued. This collection even spread to the garden which contained an even more curious assemblage – this time of living creatures. There were armadillos, a

Busy Putney Hill was just a gentle thoroughfare at the time that Swinburne came to live here with his friend Theodore Watts-Dunton. A short stroll took Swinburne up onto Putney Heath, and then Wimbledon Common beyond. Here, in the summers of his declining years, the ageing poet spent some of his happiest moments.

wombat, woodchucks, a peahen, a racoon, a kangaroo, a deer, a chameleon, a salamander, and even a zebu, a fierce little animal not much bigger than a Shetland pony, which had cost Rossetti £20. It had been a delicate business carrying the zebu through the house and out into the garden, where it was tied to a tree; and the tale is told how the animal finally tore up the tree by the roots and chased the ageing pre-Raphaelite round the garden!

Rossetti suffered from insomnia, and, to cure it, took chloral, a drug which induced in him periods of terrible gloom. At such times he depended on his friends for comfort, Walter Watts-Dunton amongst them. It was at this time that Watts-Dunton, perceiving that Swinburne was being stultified by the older man, suggested that Swinburne should go and live with him instead. Swinburne agreed to the suggestion, and so moved to Putney, to a much more conventional household where his work would not be disturbed by such eccentric influences. Here Swinburne occupied one room on the first floor, looking out on a beautiful back garden, and a bedroom on the floor above with a view through to Putney Heath. Some years later, Watts-Dunton married, and his wife has left this picture of Swinburne: 'It would be difficult to imagine a greater contrast between the idiosyncracies of two men living under the same roof than that presented by the difference between Swinburne's tidy retreat upstairs and Walter's untidy work-room downstairs. In Swinburne's room everything was in its place. At first glance the room seemed to contain little besides books . . . if he wanted to show you any particular book, he would first see that not a speck was on it. I can see him now, duster in hand, going carefully over the edges and cover to satisfy himself that all was as it should be before placing the volume in your hands.'

Here, at Putney Hill, Swinburne's life was a quiet, but regular one. He took many walks over Wimbledon Common, purchasing books at a small second-hand bookshop he had found in Wimbledon, which he would bring back and press into Watts-Dunton's hand. He was very fond of reading aloud, and his endless recitals from the works of Dickens, of whom he was particularly fond, were found tedious by the company there, since they were a nightly occurrence. Max Beerbohm has left us this vivid portrait of his visit to the house: 'While I stood talking to Watts-Dunton, talking loudly as he, for he was very deaf, I enjoyed the thrill of suspense in watching the door through which would appear Swinburne . . . Swinburne's entry for me was a great moment . . . Here, suddenly visible in the flesh, was the legendary being and divine singer . . . a strange, small figure in grey, having an air of being at once noble and roguish, proud and skittish. My name was roared to him. In shaking his hand, I bowed low, of course, a bow de coeur; and he in the old aristocratic manner, bowed equally low, but with such swiftness that we narrowly escaped concussion . . . sparse and straggling though the grey hair was that fringed the immense pale dome of his head, and venerably haloed though he was for me by his greatness, there was yet something about him – boyish? girlish? childish, rather; something of a beautifully well-bred child. But he had the eyes of a god, and the smile of an elf. In figure at first glance, he seemed almost fat, but this was merely because of the way he carried himself, with his long neck strained so tightly back that he all receded from the waist upwards . . .'

Beerbohm now tells us about the luncheon. 'As soon as the mutton had been replaced by the apple-pie, Watts-Dunton leaned forward and "Well, Algernon" he roared "How was it on the Heath today?" Swinburne who had merely inclined his ear to the question now threw back his head, uttering a sound that was like the cooing of a dove and forthwith rapidly, even so

Right: '*I want to get rid of this house*' *wrote George Eliot of this residence in Wimbledon Park Road, Southfields. She found it gloomy and oppressive, and could not wait to leave it, despite her obvious enthusiasm at moving into it only a few years earlier.*

musically, he spoke to us of his walk; spoke not in the strain of a man who had been taking his daily exercise on Putney Heath, but rather in that of a Peri who had at long last been suffered to pass through paradise. And rather than that he spoke would I say that he cooingly and flutingly sang of his experience. The wonders of this morning's wind and sun and clouds were expressed in a flow of words so right and sentences so perfectly balanced that they would have seemed pedantic had they not been clearly as spontaneous as the worldless notes of a bird song.' Alas, the singing was soon to stop. Swinburne was not a fit man, and after a winter of chills, aged 72, died on April 2 1909.

George Eliot (1819–1880) who lived at **Holly Lodge, 31 Wimbledon Park Road, SW18**, with her husband moved here in February 1859 from Richmond where she had been living for more than three years. She was aged 40, and had just published *Adam Bede*. In her journal of February 8 that year she seemed full of enthusiasms for the house. 'Yesterday' she wrote, 'we went to take possession of Holly Lodge, Wandsworth, which is to be our dwelling, we expect for years to come. It was a deliciously fresh, bright day – I will accept the omen.' Elsewhere she wrote: 'Our home is very comfortable, with far more of vulgar indulgences in it than I ever expected to have again; but you must not imagine it a snug place, just peeping above the holly bushes. Imagine it rather, as a tall cake, with a low garnish of holly and laurel. As it is we are very well off, with glorious breezy walks, and wide horizons, well ventilated rooms, and abundant water'. But the enchantment was not to last. As soon as June that same year she was writing, somewhat sourly, to a friend, 'I want to get rid of this house, cut cables and drift about. I dislike Wandsworth, and should think with unmitigated regret of our coming were it not for you'. Since her friend, Mrs Richard Congreve, was also a neighbour, this was hardly the most tactful letter to write. Especially as Mrs

Congreve seemed most happy in her own home. 'Alas', wrote George Eliot the following month, 'no one comes to take our house off our hands ... we may be forced to stay here after all.' In fact the house was disposed of, and quite soon, so the Eliots were able to move on after all. The only literary association with Holly Lodge is with *The Mill On The Floss* ... for in the dedication of the MSS. of that novel, George Eliot had written: 'To my beloved husband, George Henry Lewes, I give this MS. of my third book, written in the sixth year of our life together, at Holly Lodge, South Fields, Wandsworth, and finished 21 day of March 1860.'

Thomas Hardy (1840–1928) commemorated at **172 Trinity Road, Tooting, SW17** in the borough of Wandsworth, who lived here for three years from 1878–1881, did not much enjoy his stay either. He had taken the house on a three year lease. Hardy could never feel at home in London. He complained of a strange feeling of being near to a 'monster whose body had four million heads and eight million eyes'. He yearned for the country, and for the West Country in particular. A hint of his claustrophobia is included in his description of the dawn seen from his house in Trinity Road. 'In the upper back bedroom at daybreak; just past three o'clock. There is a golden light behind the horizon; within it are the four millions. The roofs are damp grey; the streets are still filled with night as with a dark stagnant flood whose surface brims to the top of the houses. Above the air is light. A fire or two glows in the mass. Behind are Highgate Hills . . . On the Crystal Palace Hills in the other direction a lamp is still burning up in the daylight. The lamps are also still flickering in the street and one policeman walks down as if it were noon.' From this tall, dark, and unwelcoming house Hardy settled down to the London literary life. In November 1878, *The Return of the Native* was published. While living here, he met Mathew Arnold and Tennyson.

But he was not a fit man. In the winter of 1880 he was bedridden for several weeks, only able to walk about on Wandsworth Common by the following spring. It was with a great feeling of relief that he and his wife moved away from London two years later to their new home in Dorset. The plaque was erected in 1940.

At **5 The Pavement, Clapham Common, SW11** there is a plaque to **Zacharay Macaulay** (1768–1838) the philanthropist, and his son **Thomas Macaulay** (1800–1859) the historian. Macaulay senior had returned to England in 1799 after a lengthy period of service and philanthropic work in the Caribbean. For the previous six years he had been governor of Sierra Leone, a colony of liberated slaves. He and his family moved here in 1805, although he had previously been living in rented accommodation in the area for two years. Trevelyan, Macaulay's nephew, described the house as 'a roomy, comfortable dwelling with a small garden behind, and in front a very small one indeed'. Macaulay senior was then editor of the *Christian Observer*. 'He used then, summer and winter, to rise at 5 a.m. and if in winter to light his own fire . . . The consequence was that, though a busy man, who did more perhaps than two ordinary men in a day, he never seemed to hurry.' His son, the future Lord Macaulay, was already showing outstanding academic ability. 'From the time that he was three years old', writes Trevelyan, 'he read incessantly, for the most part lying on the rug before the fire, with his book on the ground, and a piece of bread and butter in his hand . . . He did not care for toys, but was fond of taking his walk, when he would hold forth to his companion . . . telling interminable stories out of his own head, or repeating what he had been reading in language far above his years . . . While he was still the merest child he was sent as a day scholar to Mr Greaves a Yorkshireman. Mrs Macaulay explained to Tom that he must learn to study without the solace of bread and butter, to which he replied "Yes, Mama, industry shall be my bread, and attention my butter".' The future Secretary of State, it seems, was practising little more than political insincerity in saying that, for he meant not a word of it. While it may have impressed his mother, it did not commit him in the slightest into going to school willingly, which he did not. Sometimes the boy, who was fond of the privilege of private study, and the additional comforts of learning his Greek and Latin at home, had to be forced through the front door in the mornings. In 1813, young Macaulay was sent away to private school near Cambridge, and a few years later, his father, more prosperous now, was able to afford a more ample house for his growing family.

FURTHER NAMES COMMEMORATED IN WANDSWORTH

Nearby in Old Clapham, are the residences of two architects. **Sir Charles Barry** who is commemorated at **The Elms, Clapham Common North, SW4** and **John Francis Bentley** (1839–1902) at **43 The Pavement, Old Town, Clapham, SW11**. Barry (1795–1860) had his greatest memorial in London in the Houses of Parliament, which he completed in 1860. He also designed The Travellers Club in Pall Mall, 1832, and The Reform Club, also in Pall Mall, in 1840. Bentley's largest commission was the design of Westminster Cathedral.

Final plaques in Wandsworth commemorate **David Lloyd George** (1863–1945) Prime Minister, at **3 Routh Road, Wandsworth, SW18**; **Charles Spurgeon** (1834–1892) the Evangelist, at **99 Nightingale Lane, Wandsworth Common, SW12**, and finally **Captain Lawrence Oates**, who lived at **309 Upper Richmond Road, SW15**.

LAMBETH

John Ruskin (1819–1900) was just four years old when his mother and father moved to **26 Herne Hill, Norwood, SE24**, where the site of his old home is commemorated by a plaque. Ruskin himself has left a detailed and vivid picture of life in this house during his formative years. He writes in *Praeterita*, his autobiography: 'The group of which our house was the quarter consisted of two precisely stretched partner couples of Houses, gardens and all to match; still the two highest blocks of buildings seen from Norwood to the crest of the ridge; so that the house itself, three storeyed, with garrets above, commanded, in those comparatively smokeless days, a very notable view from its garret windows of the Norwood hills on one side, and the winter sunrise over them, and of the valley of the Thames on the other, with Windsor telescopically clear in the distance ... the front and back gardens were in sufficient proportion to its size. The front was richly set with old evergreen, and well grown lilac and laburnum. The rear garden was renowned for its pears, as well as having a mulberry tree, a black Kentish one, and gooseberry and blackcurrant bushes ...'

Of his education the future critic writes: 'My mother never gave me more to learn than she knew I could easily get learnt, if I set myself honestly to work, by twelve o'clock. She never allowed anything to disturb me when my task was set. If it was not said rightly by twelve o'clock, I was kept in till I knew it, and in general, even when Latin Grammar came in to supplement the Psalms, I was my own Master for at least half an hour before half past one ...' The rigours of this long and demanding day for so young a boy were enormous, and it must

have been a relief when half past three, and then four o'clock crept round, and his father, a wine importer, would soon return from work. 'When my father returned, always punctually, from his business, he dined at half past four in the front parlour, my mother sitting beside him to hear the events of the day, and give counsel and encouragement with respect to the same – chiefly, the last, for my father was apt to be vexed if orders for sherry fell the least short of their due standard, even for a day or two ... I was never present at this time, however, and only avouch what I relate by hearsay; for between four and six it would have been a grave misdemeanour in me if I so much as approached the parlour door ... In summer we were out in the garden as long as the day lasted; tea under the white heart cherry tree; or in winter, and rough weather, at six o'clock in the drawing room – I having my cup of milk, and slice of bread and butter, in a little recess, with a table in front of it, wholly sacred to me, and in which I remained in the evening as an idol in a niche, while my mother knitted and my father read to her, and to me, so far as I chose to listen ...'

Year after year the growing Ruskin accompanied his parents on long tours across England and on the Continent. He was never wholly allowed to escape his tuition from his mother, for 'as soon as I was able to read she began a course of Bible work with me, which never ceased till I went to Oxford'. Strangely, at Oxford he did not shine academically, although he took the Newdigate Prize. He was not particularly fit, and when he came down from the University he spent two years abroad, returning, once again in 1842, to the house at Herne Hill. A. Collingwood, in his *Life and Work of John Ruskin* writes of this time: 'He was very busy, writing a book. In the afternoon his careful mother would turn him out for a tramp round the Norwood Lanes ... Dinner over, another hour or two's writing, and early to bed

Near the towering might of H.M.S. 'Dreadnought's' invincible guns, the house of a ship's commander from the navy of George III is protected from any recurrence of the scurrilous mutiny that threatened the life of Captain Bligh, and the safety of his ship, the ill-fated H.M.S. 'Bounty'.

after finishing his chapter with a flourish of eloquence, to be read next morning at breakfast to his father and mother.' This work was the first volume of Ruskin's *Modern Painters* which was published in 1843, the year before the family moved away from the house where he had grown through childhood and adolescence into formidable manhood. The plaque was first erected in 1909.

Vice Admiral Bligh, Commander of the ill-fated *Bounty*, lived at **100 Lambeth Road, SE1**. He was born in Cornwall in 1754, and joined the navy at a young age. Between 1772 and 1774 he accompanied Captain Cook on his second voyage around the world, when he was dubbed 'Bread Fruit Bligh' through discovering this plant at Otaheite. Bligh was a useful officer. He was cool under attack and a first class navigator. He did have one drawback – his total lack of consideration for others, and when he was appointed Captain in Command of H.M.S. *Bounty* in 1787 it was his uncouth temperament, more than anything else, which led to the legendary mutiny. The *Bounty*, a ship of 250 tons, was on its way back to Otaheite, this time to try to obtain some healthy bread fruit plants for experimental growing purposes. But before Bligh reached the island, the mutiny had erupted, and he and 18 others were overpowered and cast off in a small boat. They had some food, but no chart, and it was only Bligh's exceptional skill as a navigator that ensured their survival. Bligh returned eventually to England to see three of the mutineers hanged, resuming his command in the Royal Navy, and going on to serve bravely under Nelson at Copenhagen in 1801, for which he received the personal thanks of the Admiral of The Fleet. He lived only briefly in this house, retiring, in part to the country, and in part to a residence in Bond Street where, in 1817, he died.

David Cox, the artist, is commemorated at **34 Foxley Road, SW9** where he lived between 1827 and 1841, though again he stayed here only sporadi-

cally. Cox's story began in Birmingham, where his father was a blacksmith, and where he was born in 1783. His first opportunity to paint came when he was given a box of colours after breaking a leg. Cox was frail. Not for him the heavy physical work required of a smithy. Instead Cox was apprenticed to the toy trade, where he painted buttons, lacquered buckles, snuff boxes and the like. A break came for him when he was asked by a friend to assist in grinding the colours for painting the scenery at The Birmingham Theatre. By this time Cox was already taking lessons under Joseph Barber (The Barber Institute in Birmingham, named after him, has one of the most superb collections of classical paintings in Britain), and was showing immense promise. This promise was quickly recognised at The Birmingham Theatre, especially by Macready, the famous actor, who was in the company, and who insisted on Cox painting the scenery of any plays in which he appeared. For two years Cox stayed with Macready, before coming for the first time to London to paint the scenery at Astley's Theatre in Lambeth. Cox was 20, and the date was 1804. At the time he was lodging with a Mrs Ragg, a widow, who had two daughters, the elder of whom Cox was later to marry. Then, they lived in a small cottage in Dulwich, on the common, and it was not until nearly 20 years later, after much travelling, and at the time being very poor, that Cox and his wife settled in the house in Foxley Road. He had still not been fully recognised by the art 'establishment', and Cox's restlessness then showed that he himself was not yet content with either his style, or the quality of work which that style permitted. It was not until he was aged 59, in 1839, that Cox began painting in oils, and found the fluency that had been eluding him for so long.

Sir Phillip Greet, the actor manager, is commemorated at **160 Lambeth Road, SE1**; John Leech (1817–1864) caricaturist, at **Stamford Street, SE1**.

This neat villa in a suburban part of Deptford, is the birthplace of Edgar Wallace (right) master crime writer. A mile away, the River Thames, so busy in the day's of Wallace's childhood, is little more than a quiet waterfront. But on a foggy morning, as the low mournful calls from vessels underway sweep across the dark water, the spine chilling cries from one of Wallace's 'victims' can still be imagined.

CAMBERWELL

Joseph Chamberlain, the statesman, was born at **188 Camberwell Grove, SE5**, in 1836. The future statesman lived in this house through the early years of his childhood before his father removed with the family to Islington. Details of his life there will be found under that section of this book (see page 100).

Annie Besant (1847–1933) the social reformer, commemorated by a plaque at **39 Colby Road, SE19**, also lived in Camberwell only briefly. Remembered especially for her organisation of the famous Matchmakers' strike in 1887, hers was a curious story. She had been educated as a girl by Miss Marryat, a sister of Captain Marryat the novelist, and in 1867, at the age of 20, married Frank Besant, a clergyman, and a younger brother of Sir Walter Besant (see Hampstead page 123). Quite suddenly, after five years of happy marriage, she lost her faith, and, as a result, felt she could no longer share the life and calling of her husband. She took her small children and came to live here in Camberwell emerging as the authoress of *Gospel of Atheism* (1878) and a champion of neo-Mathusianism. So confused was staid Victorian society by this change in her, that they deemed her unsuitable to look after her children any longer, and, as a result of a court order brought about by the father, they were returned to his care, church twice on Sundays, and prayers before each meal. When the children left her, Annie Besant became more deeply involved in her causes. She joined the Fabian Society in 1885, was present with John Burns at the Trafalgar Square riot the following year, and organised the Matchmakers' strike the year after that, also forming their union. Shortly afterwards, she became heavily in-

volved in theosophy, an influence which took her to India, where she eventually settled.

Another traveller from England was **Edgar Wallace** (1875–1932) commemorated at **6 Tressillian Crescent, Deptford, SE4**. He was born in Greenwich, the son of an actor and actress, but was brought up and cared for here by George Freeman, a Billingsgate fishporter. His gregarious nature and inquiring mind of the world beyond these dull South London streets soon showed itself, and by the age of 11 he was playing truant from school to sell newspapers in Ludgate Circus. Here, from his pavement site, the lights of the great Fleet Street newspaper offices burned a dull yellow through the London fogs. There was a bustle and excitement immensely appealing to the young boy's restless mind as he watched the hansom cabs halt outside the busy front doors of the newspaper buildings, and breathless correspondents leaped down to rush in with their copy for the early editions. Soon Wallace was working there himself, as a printer's boy, going on to become a newsboy, absorbing everything he could, yearning to play an important part in that great machine himself. As a teenager, he went to work in a shoe shop, in a mackintosh factory, on a Grimsby trawler, as a milk roundsman, a roadmaker and a builder's labourer. Eventually, yearning to travel, he joined The Royal West Kent Regiment, going to South Africa. He was already writing, having contributed some songs to a comedian Arthur Roberts before he left England, and after the Boer War was over, he stayed on in the colony writing articles for *The Cape Times*, before becoming Reuter's correspondent there, as well as working for the *Daily Mail*. Years later, a grand man in journalism, he was one of the most respected people in Fleet Street. The memories, though, of his early childhood days in Deptford never left him, and the imagery of that landscape and zest of the people gave him rich background material for his thrillers.

Philip Earl of Chesterfield and Viscount Wolseley are both commemorated by plaques for their stay of residence at the Ranger's House, Blackheath. This elegant mansion is now owned by the Greater London Council, and is open to the public.

GREENWICH & BLACKHEATH

At the **Ranger's House, Blackheath, SE10** two people are commemorated. **Philip Earl of Chesterfield** (1694–1773) retired here at the end of his life, and **Wolseley**, the **First Viscount Chesterfield** (1833–1913) lived here for a time in the final decade of the nineteenth century. It was in 1748, when Chesterfield resigned as Secretary of State, that he took up the opportunity of developing the Ranger's House as a summer retreat from his residence in South Audley Street. Too deaf to enjoy society any longer, and crippled with goutish rheumatism, he found country life more and more suited to him. In 1753 he wrote to a friend, 'I am now, for the first time in my life, impatient for the summer, that I may go and hide myself at Blackheath, and converse with my vegetables'. These 'conversations' were held particularly with melons and pineapples, which he delighted in cultivating. It was from this house that many of Chesterfield's *Letters to His Son* were written, which, had the boy taken the worldly wisdom and advice contained therein, would surely have fitted him for high office. These letters are a model of how the successful statesman should conduct his affairs. That, at least, was Chesterfield's opinion. In fact, the boy's childhood was so robbed of the freedom to make mistakes, and profit by them, that he turned out to be everything Lord Chesterfield had hoped to avoid. On one occasion Lord Chesterfield had invited several of his friends to dinner, with the intention of showing off his son's accomplishments. 'The youth', George Hill wrote in his 1891 *Introduction to Lord Chesterfield's Worldly Wisdom*, 'was unfor-

tunately so delighted with a cherry tart, that after he had demolished the crust and fruit, unwilling to lose any of the juice, he cleared his plate by lapping or licking it up, so that the chin, mouth and lips were besmeared. Never perhaps was his father more mortified. He recovered himself, however, so far as to tell his son's servant that his master wanted shaving'. The son continued to embarrass Lord Chesterfield. He ran up large debts, married secretly, and finally, died young.

No such embarrassment bothered Wolseley during his time at the Ranger's House. After a distinguished period as a front line officer, in which, amongst other triumphs, he led the expedition to relieve Gordon at Khartoum, he was appointed Adjutant General. He was offered the Ranger's House by Queen Victoria in 1888, and lived here respectably until he retired from the army a few years later.

Another military association with Blackheath comes through **Macartney House**, in **Greenwich Park, SE10**, where **General Wolfe**, the victor of Quebec is commemorated. The house belonged to Wolfe's parents, who had purchased it in 1751 for £3000. Wolfe, then a Lieutenant Colonel, and only 24, spent many leaves in this house which he called 'the prettiest situated house in England'. While his parents were away, Wolfe made full use of the house before going to Quebec in early 1759, where he was killed in action. **Nathaniel Hawthorne** (1804–1864) the American author, stayed at **4 Pond Road, Blackheath** for a time, and **Charles Gounod** (1818–1893) the composer stayed at **15 Morden Road, Blackheath, SE3**. **Samuel Smiles**, commemorated at **11 Granville Park, Lewisham, SE13**, was the author of *Self Help*, one of the publishing phenomena of the nineteenth century. Smiles, who was born in 1812, was a zealous social reformer. After a career as a newspaper editor with the *Leeds Times*, and then in railway management, his first publishing success was with his biography of Robert Stephenson, published in 1857. This

Below and right: *Macartney House, once the home of General Wolfe, is a large rambling house which now forms several separate residences. Standing on the edge of Blackheath, it commands fine views over Greenwich Park, the Observatory, Royal Naval College, and the Thames.*

turned into a minor best seller for those days. After writing it, he turned to lecturing, and it was as a result of this contact with the working man that he realised how sorely they were in need of a simple manual in which basic information for their own betterment was given. *Self Help* was the title he gave to the book, and it was published in 1859. Within five years over 50,000 copies had been sold. Within a further five this amount had trebled. In 1866 he moved to this house in Blackheath, living here until 1874 when he moved to Kensington. He died in 1904.

Finally, in South London, **Sir James Clark**, the polar explorer, who lived from 1800 until 1862, is remembered at **2 Eliot Place, Blackheath, SE13**.

Below: *Nathaniel Hawthorne stayed for a short while in this large, spacious house set in very peaceful surroundings in Pond Road, off the South Side of Blackheath.*

BIBLIOGRAPHY

Bell, Clive *Virginia Woolf* (1972) Hogarth

Bell, Clive Interview in *The Guardian* (1972)

Briggs, Asa *The History of Broadcasting in the United Kingdom* (Vol. 1 1961, vol. 2 1965, vol. 3 1970) Oxford University Press

Chaplin, Charles *My Autobiography* (1964) Bodley Head

Dictionary of National Biography Oxford University Press

Gaunt, William *Kensington and Chelsea* (1975) Batsford

Grahame, Kenneth *First Whisper of Wind in the Willows* Edited by Elspeth Grahame (1944) Methuen

Hardwick, Michael and Mollie *The Charles Dickens Companion* (1965) John Murray

Harvey, Sir Paul *Oxford Companion to English Literature* (1967) Oxford University Press

Hill, George *The Worldly Wisdom of Lord Chesterfield* (1891)

Holroyd, Michael *Review of Virginia Woolf by Clive Bell* in *The Times* (June 12 1972)

Hone, Joseph *William Butler Yeats* (1971) Penguin Books

Jones, Sydney *Thames Triumphant* (1943) Studio Publications

Kent, William *Encyclopaedia to London* (1951) J. M. Dent

London County Council *Survey of London*, and various London County Council pamphlets on houses of historic interest.

Moore, Harry T. *The Intelligent Heart – The Story of D. H. Lawrence* (1960) Penguin Books

Mottram, R. H. *John Galsworthy* (1963) Longman Group

Pearson, Hesketh *Oscar Wilde* (1946) Penguin Books

Priestly, J. B. *The Edwardians* (1972) Heinemann

Swinnerton, Frank *Bookman's London* (1972) Garnstone Press

The Shorter Oxford English Dictionary (1975) Oxford University Press

Picture Sources
The photographs of houses and introductory
shots for the three main sections of the book
were specially taken by Julian Plowright.
The sources for other photographs are listed
below and both the author and the publishers
would like to acknowledge the help of those
who have lent photographs and given
permission for their reproduction in this
book:

The Radio Times Hulton Picture Library:
Promenaders in Kensington Gardens p8,
Brunel p15, Whistler p16, Carlyle p16, Oscar
Wilde p20, Thackeray p24–25, J. S. Mill p26,
W. H. Hunt p29, Millais p32, Henry James p34,
Jenny Lind p35, Benjamin Franklin p49,
Handel p48, Gladstone p52, Kitchener p53,
Nelson p54, Dr Johnson p58–59. H. G. Wells
p61, Elizabeth Barrett Browning p67, Boswell
p69, James Morse p82, Lytton Strachey p91,
William Morris p93, Virginia Woolf p92,
Randolph Churchill p96–97, Little Tich p105,
George Leybourne p104, 106, Albert Chevalier
p106, Charles Dickens p109, 110, Charles
Darwin p112, John Constable p124, William
Friese Green p126, D. H. Lawrence p127,
Sigmund Freud p127, Gandhi p131, Robert
Falcon Scott p136, Edgar Wallace 146.

The National Portrait Gallery:
Kipling p50, Disraeli p52, Pepys p53, Turner
p57, Trollope p80, Spencer Perceval p95,
James Barrie p97, Charles Dickens p109, John
Keats p117, 119.

Raymond Manders and Joe Mitchenson:
Collins Music Hall p103.

Drawings by Aubrey Beardsley were
reproduced from *The Later Works of Aubrey
Beardsley* Dover Publications (1967).

INDEX